Surviving
History

*The Life of B.Y. Harris
in East Tennessee*

Marilyn Layman Mascaro

outskirtspress
DENVER, COLORADO

Surviving History
The Life of B.Y. Harris in East Tennessee
All Rights Reserved.
Copyright © 2015 Marilyn Layman Mascaro
v2.0 r2.0

Outskirts Press, Inc.
http://www.outskirtspress.com

ISBN: 978-1-4787-4322-4

Library of Congress Control Number: 2014916601

Outskirts Press and the "OP" logo are trademarks belonging to Outskirts Press, Inc.

PRINTED IN THE UNITED STATES OF AMERICA

Contents

Dedication

THE MOMENT UNFOLDED at my childhood home in Knox County, Tennessee. My grandmother and her sister had journeyed across two counties while towing four beds from their mother's estate. Being ten years old, I didn't question Great-Aunt Elsie's presence at this event. Her childless state contributed to her being the family historian, but she wasn't my grandmother's only sibling. What machinations occurred to have the beds brought to my family, among all the cousins, are lost now. Certainly my grandmother noted that the estate contained four beds and my family four children. In any case, the furniture's disassembled pieces currently cluttered our living room and held everyone's attention.

The adults determined that we children would choose a bed in order of our ages. Therefore, Doug, my older and only brother, would pick first, then me, and then my sisters, Linda and Sherri, the six minutes that separated them now crucial. Since I usually felt overwhelmed in conflicts with my older brother and twin sisters, I silently celebrated my place in the lineup. Going second gave me a chance.

Most of the beds looked impressive. All four had solid backboards with matching but less elaborate footboards. One dark walnut specimen towered above the others, and a second was cunningly carved with leaves and flowers in what I now recognize as the Eastlake style. The third glowed with then-popular golden oak. These were all regular-sized, with the same dimensions as my parents' bed. Compared to the others, the fourth bed seemed an outcast, so different it had to be carefully talked up by the older women. Its curving headboard, for example, culminated in a cutout circle noticeably cruder than the machine-made carvings of the others. The bed's size fell somewhere between a twin and a regular, inciting a fair amount of commentary.

"Maybe people were smaller then," ventured my mother.

Plus, there were other issues. The wood was unidentifiable, even for women raised in rural East Tennessee.

"That might be oak," my grandmother ventured.

"Or chestnut," said Aunt Elsie. "And it's constructed with wooden pegs instead of nails," she added encouragingly.

By the time my brother walked importantly to make his choice, my breath was ragged. As a middle child I seemed to rarely receive my most fervent wishes, and the superior bed was so ragingly obvious to me I knew Doug would pick it. I closed my eyes and willed him otherwise. When I heard him say "this one" and looked to see his hand on the tall, black headboard, glorious breath came back to me. Sprinting across the room, I grabbed onto the odd-sized bed.

"This one is mine."

"Are you sure?" my mother asked carefully. "It's plain."

"But it's handmade," I replied, running my hand over the curved headboard.

Even I saw my grandmother and her sister glance at each other and grin.

That moment as a child eventually propelled me to this one, to writing B.Y. Harris' story while that same bed shares the room with my computer. Over the years I purchased two specially made mattress sets for it, slept in it myself, and later allowed a son that honor. Lest I forget its primitive glory, during a yard sale one customer so insisted I sell it to her out of storage in my garage that I immediately carted it into the house, where it dominated my closet for a decade.

Practicality aside, its continuing presence provides a tangible connection to my East Tennessee ancestors, a link that probably traces to B.Y. himself.

My long-deceased great-aunt, Elsie Winkels Samsel, cared enough about that connection to see for herself if a child could understand its significance. I know this because moments after I chose the family heirloom as a child, she abruptly started to cry.

To Great-Aunt Elsie…may our bed travel forward through time with its history intact.

Bartlett Yancy (B.Y.) Harris

CHAPTER 1

Bean's Station

THE BOY STRUGGLES to carry a kettle of embers scooped from the morning fire. The wire handle bites into his hand, and even when set on his family's moving wagon, the cast-iron pot needs watching. After all, in 1835 no medical facilities exist on the road to Tennessee, and these embers can burn or even disfigure a child. But the coals' value outweighs their hazard, enabling the travelers to quickly establish that night's camp and then enjoy supper. At the end of a day spent crossing mountains on foot, hunger battles fatigue within every immigrant.

This childhood journey deeply impresses the boy, and years later Bartlet Yancy Harris tells his descendents about that trail west and the job he fulfilled as an eight-year-old (1).

The adults in Bart's life carefully contemplated the move to Tennessee before committing to it. He travels with his parents, David and Polly Harris, four older siblings, and three younger ones. His uncle Thomas Harris and Thomas' family are also emigrating, giving the children cousins as well as siblings for company. Bart's parents were born in Pittsylvania County, Virginia, where their families had lived for a generation. As a young man, David proudly served in the Virginia Militia during the War of 1812 (2) then returned home to marry Polly (3). The couple settled in Virginia and welcomed their first five children, including Bart, who was born in November of 1826 (4). Next his parents moved just over the state line into nearby North Carolina, bought a farm, and produced three more children. So in many ways they enjoyed both security and prosperity before this journey.

But in the early 19th century, restless Americans constantly move westward. David and Polly know relocating will improve their prospects because of the plentiful, cheap land waiting to the west. They purchase a Conestoga wagon, a variety sturdy enough to survive rough roads and mountainous terrain, and carefully plan the three-hundred-mile trip. Even though the men will hunt for game along the trail, the families must bring basic food supplies for the journey and all essential possessions for their new farms such as tools and livestock. Soon the Harrises sell their property and say difficult goodbyes to family in Virginia. After all, they will never return. The trip begins in the spring with the arrival of warm weather.

With only four adults but ten children in the group, all but the youngest travelers shoulder responsibilities. After all, lost animals or broken equipment could delay their establishing homes before the winter.

The families' destination lies in upper East Tennessee: Bean Station in Grainger County. This small town rests on the western edge of the Tennessee Valley, close to the Cumberland Mountains. By 1835 it had thrived for over half a century. Similar to most frontier towns, Bean Station developed near a river, but it also spans two crucial early roads. One route began as a buffalo path and effortlessly runs north/south with the Tennessee Valley. In contrast, Daniel Boone developed the east-to-west road in the late eighteenth century because early settlers needed a route through the Cumberland Mountains to Kentucky and beyond. Soon after Boone's success, sons of his friend William Bean established a fort and stagecoach station where the two roads cross. Naturally the settlement became known as Bean's Station. It evolved into one of the era's busiest trading posts and stagecoach stations, an essential stop between Baltimore and New Orleans, North Carolina and Kentucky.

The area outside of town contains possibilities too. Nearby the Holston River flows southward toward Knoxville, providing fish to eat, water for animals, and transportation for durable goods. Foothills covered with forests fill the region, supplying both timber and firewood. Farmable land exists too, although much of it must first be logged. The area teems with natural resources and enduring wilderness.

ゝゝゝ

At some point during the summer of 1835, Bart and his family arrive at their upper East Tennessee destination, having successfully crossed the Appalachian Mountains. They quickly begin establishing households and farms. David and Polly settle several miles west of Bean Station on the north side of Clinch Mountain because land costs less there. The family moves into two attached cabins called a double home, and in 1836 David first pays taxes in his new state (5). He farms to feed his family, raises tobacco for cash, and only buys essentials that can't be made or grown. During these early years in Tennessee, the family enjoys fine health, and two more children are born, James (Jim), who Polly was pregnant with on the journey from Virginia, and Richard (6). Eight-year-old Bart settles easily into his new home. Work consumes a settler's day, even when a child, but Bart eats well and has time to play. Plus he likes Tennessee, finding the ridges more exciting than the flatter land in Virginia. Upon hearing the local legend that Daniel Boone was the first white man in the region, Bart's favorite game involves reenacting the frontiersman's historic feat with his brothers.

When the Harrises do need to trade or buy goods, the venture takes most of a day because they must cross Clinch Mountain to reach Bean Station. One Saturday morning nine-year-old Bart accompanies his father to the busy crossroads. His siblings stay at home, so he escapes the bossy demands of the older children and the constant questions of the younger ones. As their wagon emerges from the hills west of the settlement, David and Bart first pass unpainted wooden homes, then a stable, then several whitewashed houses. On the main roads oxen pull wagons loaded with vegetables, or they wait stoically near a mercantile while their owners sell goods to the merchants. Some travelers just pass through Bean Station while heading toward larger towns such as Rogersville or Knoxville. The road east to the Holston River dock thrives also, even though water provides slow transportation usually reserved for lumber and settlers.

While David trades, Bart admires the store's selection of hard candy and other merchandise. He then waits nearby, fidgeting through his father's conversation with the owner. Finally David tells him to check on the wagon. While Bart waits outside, he hears the jangle of a coming stagecoach and soon spies a team of horses pulling it over the alternating trenches and clumps of clay that comprise the road. These vehicles pass through town three times a week, stopping to exchange passengers, mail, and cargo (7). Before the stage can tackle Clinch Mountain, which is only the first of many imposing obstacles in the Cumberland range, draft animals will be replaced and gear repaired.

After the coach stops, its passengers exit and stretch

their cramped limbs. Remembering how he trudged over mountain trails on his journey to Tennessee, Bart isn't particularly sympathetic to their grumbling. But when he notices several men head toward the town's taverns, his stomach twinges. Breakfast was hours ago.

Luckily for Bart, his father's trips to town almost always include a midday meal at one of Bean Station's three inns. These establishments rent rooms to pass-ersby and serve food and spirits. After David finishes his business in the store, he and Bart head toward the town's largest tavern, the Whiteside Inn, which was built early in Bean Station's history. Originally a two-story log building, over the years as business in-creased the Whiteside brothers built a brick addition, included a post office, and created the largest stage-coach tavern between New Orleans and Washington D.C. Many famous Americans stayed there, such as Davy Crockett and Andrew Jackson, or worked there, such as Nancy Hanks, Abraham Lincoln's mother (8).

Bart admires the tavern for its intriguing atmo-sphere and filling food, so once inside he willingly overlooks the stuffy interior. David soon begins talk-ing with the other customers in a conversation domi-nated by one subject. A decade earlier, Tennesseans had elected Davy Crockett to the U.S. Congress as a political ally of President Jackson. But when the congressman spoke against the president's plan to force the Cherokee Indians out of the southeast, the men's friendship ended. Most Americans agreed with

Jackson's aggressive policy, and Crockett was unsuccessful at stopping the removals. When Tennesseans didn't re-elect him to Congress, he moved west to the Texas territory. A few months before Bart's trip to town, Crockett died at the Alamo while fighting for Texas' independence from Mexico. Not everyone in the tavern agrees with Crockett's lenient Indian policy, as they describe it, but many remember him personally and fondly.

In fact, the saga in Texas still rages. Another East Tennessee native, General Sam Houston, currently leads an army there against the Mexicans. The tavern's customers vigorously debate his chances of success. Bart likes hearing about Crockett's last stand at the Alamo because he admires the courage and resourcefulness of the men who died there. He proudly claims them and Daniel Boone as his heroes. But the conversation becomes too complicated for him to follow. David is an educated man and a veteran who has well-considered ideas on how best to support Texas. Bart soon thinks longingly of home.

❧❧❧

By the late 1830s David moves his family to the south side of Clinch Mountain, closer to the Holston River and the crossroads at Bean Station. A secondary road runs nearby and crosses into Hawkins County near the small town of Mooresburg. The Harrises soon begin meeting their new neighbors, including one elderly couple, John Lebow and his wife Katherine. As a young man Lebow came from Pennsylvania and fought the Indians with Tennessee's frontier militia, first serving in 1793 under the command of Stokley Donaldson and eventually becoming an ensign in 1797 (9). After his years in the military, Lebow settled in Tennessee and bought large amounts of land, including fifty acres in a prime location outside of Bean Station (10). By the time the Harrises meet him, the neighborhood considers him a local treasure.

The Lebows host the first Independence Day celebration that Bart and his family attend in Grainger County. The grandeur of the couple's house and farm so impacts the twelve-year-old that later in life he vividly remembers first seeing them (11). As a child, such wealth impresses. The huge meal served at the gathering includes smoked ham, green beans, cornbread, and a considerable selection of cakes and pies. But Bart's father David frowns at the slaves he sees serving this food; after all, most families in the area, including his own, hold anti-slavery beliefs. Lebow, in contrast, owns nine slaves (12).

After dinner, the adults share farming techniques and gossip. Lebow reminisces about his adventures on the frontier, and a few other men share stories of the Revolution. Later the children play hide and seek among the farm's many outbuildings and trees. Bart loves these games. He can't outrun older brother Thomas or his fourteen-year-old sister Mary, but he excels among his own age group and thrives at the competition. Two of Lebow's granddaughters, Lucretia and Mary, are near Bart's age and enjoy the games too. When the McAnally and Long children join in, shrieks and yelling can be heard throughout the gathering.

When John Lebow dies in 1840, many community members mourn with his family and attend the funeral at the family cemetery in Grainger County. His son-in-law William Gray accepts the important job of executor of estate. Lebow's holdings total over seventeen thousand dollars, comparable to over ten million modern dollars in terms of income value and economic status (13). His extensive acreage, farm, and general household effects are sold, with the resulting cash distributed among his wife and children. In turn they purchase much of his land, dozens of farming tools, and several different herds of livestock. Family members inherit his prized horses and more personal possessions such as bedsteads, chests, and a bureau (14). They apparently claim the slaves also.

᠉᠉᠉

Now firmly established on the south side of Clinch Mountain in Grainger County, David adds land speculation to his other endeavors. He buys land, logs it with the help of his sons and hired men, and then either sells or farms the cleared acres. Unfortunately logging is hazardous work, and at age fourteen, Bart sustains a serious injury while driving a sled pulled by

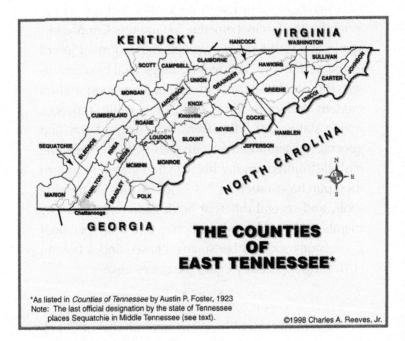

THE COUNTIES OF EAST TENNESSEE*

*As listed in *Counties of Tennessee* by Austin P. Foster, 1923
Note: The last official designation by the state of Tennessee places Sequatchie in Middle Tennessee (see text).

©1998 Charles A. Reeves, Jr.

a team of horses. As he guides the animals across a stream in an area previously logged, one of the sled's runners strikes a fallen sapling half hidden in the mud. The pole-like tree bows forward, then snaps back, striking Bart and fracturing his left leg between the knee and ankle (15). He falls back into the water, losing control of the horses and sled. Luckily his brother William sees the accident, drags him out of the creek, and rushes to find help while Bart lies moaning on the ground. David carries his unconscious son home and sends for a doctor. Since a fracture such as this one could leave Bart an invalid, the doctor stresses that he must stay immobile for several months so the leg can set properly.

But teenage boys detest inaction, and Bart resists, snapping angrily at his siblings when they encourage him. His frustration mounts because he knows that with this injury, he will never be the strongest or most agile man in the community. Bart despairs over a future he sees as disintegrating. Eventually David talks with his son, telling him that physical flaws can be overcome with cleverness, attention to detail, and honesty. Bart excels at arithmetic, which David points out can be applied to farming. After all, he says, successful farmers are often businessmen. Thankfully the break heals fairly well, but Bart will forever have a slight limp. Just as important, the reflection caused by his injury alters the direction of his life.

In fact, several of David and Polly's sons make

crucial choices during these years. Oldest brother Thomas' wild streak renders him undependable, and after his leg heals, Bart's responsibilities on the farm increase. He and William, his younger brother by just two years, essentially become David's apprentices. Bart likes the work, but he also daydreams about the future when he might run a store or build a sawmill. William, who struggled while learning to read, loves farming and can't imagine why anyone would take time away from it to mess with books or ledgers. Only Booker, the younger brother after William, finds life in Tennessee dissatisfying. At age twenty he moves to Illinois, close to his mother's family. Much like the two Harris brothers immigrated to Tennessee, three of Polly's brothers moved to Illinois. Soon Booker marries a cousin, Eliza Lansford (16). This relationship concerns the extended family, but when the marriage doesn't last, genuine scandal erupts. Booker eventually abandons his wife, creating a serious rift between him and his parents. Modern records reveal that he marries again, is drafted by the Union Army, and leads a long life (17), but after his late twenties he has no contact with his parents and siblings.

Others in David Harris' family, however, enjoy life in Tennessee as they mature during the 1840's. The younger children attend school (18) while the older siblings begin establishing independent lives. Daughter Mary weds Almarine Wynkel, who, even for the time period, has an adventurous spirit. After a few years of marriage, he leaves to fight in the Mexican-American War, an extension of the conflict over Texas that has the two countries battling for control of western lands (19). Eventually the American army marches into Mexico City, defeats General Santa Anna's army, and captures Mexico City. The war's primary purpose is gaining territory, but many Americans consider this a worthy goal, and the soldiers, Almarine included, return home as heroes.

Since the move to Tennessee, through hard work and industry, David and Polly Harris' fortunes have improved. They decide to purchase a final farm, one well-placed and prosperous enough to secure them in old age. A property comes up for sale that is just what they envision: Lebow's homestead. David purchases two adjoining parcels of land on the Hawkins/Grainger County line that include Lebow's farm and total almost three hundred acres (20). The property contains a large cabin, smokehouse, and sturdy barn; a spring provides fresh water, and its springhouse keeps food cool, even in the summer. Pasture and orchards cover the rolling hills while timber blankets the ridge across the lane. Tucked within the ridges on the south side of Clinch Mountain, the homestead rests amid a rolling valley of lush green.

CHAPTER 2

Name Change

THE 1850S BRING economic prosperity to much of the United States, and with their access to fertile farmland, timber, and transportation, the Harris family thrives also. During this decade a railroad is completed through Grainger County, providing quick access to larger retail centers for those who live near the route. The Harrises do. But rail fares are expensive, so many locals still travel the original roads through Bean Station to take their fruits and vegetables north to the town of Rogersville or south to Morristown and Knoxville. With so much opportunity, the local farmers plant additional crops. David Harris expands his holdings, buying and selling land in order to acquire exactly the farmland he wants. In 1853 he purchases over eleven hundred acres in the German Creek area of Grainger County (1). His primary cash crop, tobacco, thrives in the local climate. As his children marry, most of them live on his land and farm these extensive holdings (2). Like most East Tennessee farmers, David avoids slave labor.

For her part, Polly serves huge meals of home-grown produce and farm-raised meats to fuel her family. Oldest daughters Elizabeth and Rebecca help her with the many household chores and also assist the local midwife. Gregarious teenagers Susan and Jim attend school, as does Richard, a towheaded ten-year-old. In fact, the family coloring tends toward fairness with Bart, William, and Jim all sporting fair skin, blue eyes, and light-colored hair (3). At age twenty, Bart still limps from his teenage injury, an inconvenient but inevitable fact. The leg might slow him in speed, but it doesn't interfere with his body strength or farming ability. He and William labor on their father's farm and also work for hire, saving money for their own land. In their leisure time, they travel about the region, joking with their peers and frequenting the Bean Station tavern so often that Bart keeps a running tab there. The brothers enjoy conversing with Bean Station's young women and also visit Mooresburg in Hawkins County, where the Harrises often trade and where John Lebow's daughter Mary lives with her husband, William Gray.

By this time the Harris and Gray families have lived in the same region for fifteen years and know each other well, but their values differ. William Gray owns eight slaves, most of them children of a middle-aged couple (4), and considers his home a small planta-tion. Born in South Carolina, he lacks the usual East Tennessean's disdain for that lifestyle. He also owns two hundred acres of land, almost all of it farmable, and all the expected livestock: a herd of cows, dozens of sheep and pigs (5). But Gray most enjoys his sta-ble of a half-dozen horses. Because of horse racing's popularity, Bean Station boasts a thriving track where Gray and other affluent locals watch their horses race. Betting abounds amid the owners and bystanders in the boisterous and sometimes whiskey-fueled track atmosphere.

Of course Gray loves his family too. Of his and Mary's many offspring, their four youngest daughters still live at home, namely Mary, Lucretia, Sarah, and Margaret (6).

Because of their wealth and status, the commu-nity enjoys speculating on who the Gray sisters will marry. Twenty-five-year-old Lucretia, in particular, possesses glossy black hair and dark eyes that draw numerous suitors (7). Even amid her undeniable charms, Bart remembers her as a loud adolescent playing tag, running from him at dusk on a summer's evening. He finds her deeply striking and knows she likes him, but with this knowledge his confidence ends. Does she find him attractive? Would she pos-sibly marry him? He doesn't know. After all, his family lives comfortably, but the Grays possess real wealth. Even more worrisome, around Lucretia his limp feels more conspicuous, more of a liability. But years of farming have made Bart strong, and years of ignoring the limp have made him determined. After a few awkward conversations during which he and Lucretia gradually clarify their feelings for each other, she tacitly agrees to wait on marriage. For a while. Determined to prove himself to her father, Bart lives with his parents and saves money until he is almost twenty-six. He also assists William Gray with his tobacco crop. The planter sees ability and ambition in Bart; Bart finds in Gray a mentor for skills beyond the farming his own father taught him. Soon the two men develop a mutual trust. Finally Bart explains his prospects and asks for Lucretia's hand.

The nuptials of Bartlet Yancy Harris and Lucretia Ann Gray occur on September 23rd of 1852. They wed at William Gray's Hawkins County home in an elaborate fall ceremony (8). The economy is excellent, so guests are in the mood for celebration. The day sparkles with promise as couples dance, some more gracefully than others, but all in fun. In the middle of the party the newlyweds stroll out to the backyard under the shade trees and momentarily watch Gray's prized black colt as it frolics over the foothills. Bart tells Lucretia about a wedding gift he ordered from a cabinetmaker, a bed crafted in the style of the day, high off the floor and with a curving headboard. In the crisp autumn air he places his hands on his bride's waist and draws her toward him. They kiss until the fall coolness dissipates and an eager yearning replaces it. Now their life together truly begins.

Bart and Lucretia settle into marriage as easily as any young couple. They live near Bean Station in Grainger County where he farms and helps his father-in-law with his crops, particularly tobacco. The two men soon grasp that selling the crop to middlemen in larger towns severely cuts into their profits. Therefore they enter the tobacco-processing business, allowing them greater control over costs. Lucretia's routine resembles her lifestyle from before marriage, as she often socializes with other women in town. By early spring, though, her life changes significantly when she realizes she is pregnant. That evening after she blurts out the news to her husband, he draws her onto his lap at the dinner table. She laughs at such foolishness, then, as they smile at each other, decides the baby should inherit her husband's kind blue eyes.

Before long the Harris/Gray connection strengthens when Bart's younger brother William marries Lucretia's sister Mary (9). Both families applaud this second union, and another festive wedding occurs. William and Mary settle in Hawkins County near Mooresburg, close to her parents. But William maintains his independence from his in-laws. After the wedding, when Mary moves into their new home, she brings with her a personal servant, a slave. Having known the woman since birth, Mary considers her a friend and confidant. Privately horrified, William carefully explains his belief that they should provide for themselves and not profit from slave labor (10). The servant soon returns to Mary's parents.

By 1860 Bart and Lucretia have been married eight years. Marriage and parenthood have propelled them into adulthood and stability. The thirty-three-year-old Bart discards his childhood name and uses his initials instead: B.Y. He considers the new title more fitting for an ambitious businessman.

B.Y. and Lucretia's household thrives with two active sons, six-year-old Will, who already attends school, and two-year-old Tommy (11). A daughter, Mary Louisa, will be born in July (12). A thirteen-year-old white girl lives with them and helps Lucretia with housework (13). With Lucretia's family connections and her husband's hard work and initiative, their finances have flourished. William Gray provides the capital for the tobacco-processing business, but B.Y. oversees the daily operations, keeping meticulous records. In addition to an account book, he fills out a daily ledger, carefully noting sales that range from minor plugs of tobacco to large-scale transactions.

B.Y.'s customers usually pay with cash or by trading tobacco, but they also barter items such as shoes or bushels of corn. Fredrick Wynkel, father of B.Y.'s brother-in-law Almarine, trades four bedsteads to settle his debt, while Almarine himself tends to barter pints of whisky (14). This tobacco business enjoys overwhelming success, and in 1860 B.Y.'s personal worth stands at over three thousand dollars (15), giving him the economic status of over $850,000 in modern dollars and making him one of the wealthiest men in Grainger County (16). B.Y. farms but he also oversees his interests in town and even after marriage occasionally raises a pint at the Bean Station Tavern. After all, local business transactions occur there as well as the sharing of information and opinions. B.Y.'s goal of personal success includes being well-known and trusted in the region. Well on his way toward meeting this goal, his unfolding life meets every expectation, every desire, he contemplated as a youth.

With two marriages and a shared business between them, the Harris and Gray families interact frequently. Still, they are greatly amused when Harris son Jim quite obviously falls for the youngest Gray daughter, Margaret. Their courtship entertains the community and Jim's friends near and far. Newlyweds William and Mary receive a letter from Jack Lansford, William and Jim's cousin who teaches school in Illinois. Jack asks the couple to remind Jim to write him a letter and "not be so slow." Jack adds, "For if he is as slow when he goes a courting as he is about writing I am sure he will never get a wife" (17). But Jim reveals himself as more resourceful than his cousin Jack gives him credit for, and he and twenty-two-year-old Margaret soon marry (18). At the wedding the only unmarried Harris brother, twenty-year-old Richard, jokingly claims that he deserves a Gray girl for himself. There is, in fact, one daughter near his age who didn't marry one of his brothers. She is a widow…at age twenty-three.

After marrying, Jim and Margaret live with the Grays in the elderly couple's elegant home. With B.Y. overseeing Gray's tobacco crop, and slaves and tenants providing the farm's manual labor, Jim's days are leisurely. He becomes a gentleman farmer like his father-in-law and spends time reading, visiting the stables, and handling some of the farm's bookkeeping. This appalls his older brother William, who teases him relentlessly about being too refined to plow a field. In spite of such good-natured ribbing, the bonds between the three brothers only strengthen because of their wives' family ties.

ﻟﻟﻟ

Thus the move to East Tennessee pays off handsomely for David and Polly Harris. Their ten children all live into adulthood, a feat accomplished by good nutrition, wise decisions, and a healthy dose of luck. Living comfortably on their productive farm, the couple have the joy of being grandparents many times over. Most of their daughters live nearby with their families since their husbands tenant farm for David (19). So does their oldest son, Thomas. Youngest son Richard soon finishes school and makes plans to explore the Indian Territory with his cousin Jack. They will travel throughout the west and hunt game in the Rocky Mountains. But for now the thriving family sees each other often at informal get-togethers and meals.

Hopefully the Harrises appreciate this time of prosperity and togetherness. It soon ends abruptly when they become firsthand participants in one of America's most horrific events.

CHAPTER 3

The War Begins at Home

OF ALL THE regions that experience turmoil during the Civil War, East Tennessee withstands chaos as profound as any. Tensions continually fester because supporters of both Union and Confederacy live near each other throughout the war. Armies and guerrilla groups from both sides occupy the region, which partially explains why the population withstands four years of crime, violence, and armed conflict. But East Tennessee doesn't just experience a military war that wrecks the economy; its society disintegrates also. Divisiveness and brutality abound, and like many other families, the Harrises of Grainger County find themselves immersed in the uproar.

After the other Southern states secede from the Union, Tennesseans vote on whether or not to join them. This vote spotlights the cultural and economic differences within the state's regions. The middle and west areas have flatter land and more navigable rivers than in the east. These circumstances allow for larger farms and plantations using slave labor to grow cotton. The state government resides in Middle Tennessee and intertwines with this slave-owning culture. East Tennessee, with its hills and mountains, contains smaller farms that grow tobacco, a crop that doesn't require as much labor as cotton. As these differences solidify across decades, they spawn deep conflicts that simmer in the prewar political atmosphere.

When citizens vote on secession, the eastern counties decide against this drastic step, but the rest of the state elects to leave the Union, and Tennessee secedes on June 8, 1861. Men from the eastern counties soon meet, and then ask the Confederate State of Tennessee for permission to create a separate state. Their request is denied.

Even though David Harris, his wife Polly, and most of their children were born in Virginia, they support the Union and abhor slavery. In March of 1861 cousin Jack Lansford from Illinois writes his uncle David about Abe Lincoln's 1860 Republican Party platform. Jack refers David to the platform's second and eighth articles, which state the party's stance on slavery (1). The eighth article denies the legal existence of slavery and the second quotes the Declaration of Independence that "all men are created equal." David already agrees with these views. In Abe Lincoln the two men have found a politician they can support.

As William clarified when he insisted his bride set up housekeeping without slave labor, the Harrises do not condone slavery.

On the other hand, along with many others in the region, they experience conflicting loyalties. B.Y., William and Jim's father-in-law owns slaves and follows the planter mode of wealth. William Gray's personal property compares to over two million dollars in modern economic status (2), making him one of the region's wealthiest men (3). With Jim living in the Gray household and B.Y. in business with his father-in-law, the two families enjoy close ties. The brothers often visit the Grays' home for meals with their wives' family, meals served by slaves.

Other local families also encounter these complex realities. While only about ten percent of East Tennesseans own slaves, some non-slave owners have Confederate sympathies. This includes many in the Mooresburg area, where the Grays live. These families consist of William's neighbors, B.Y.'s friends, and their wives' childhood companions. In fact sympathy with the Southern cause so dominates in Mooresburg that at the war's outset men from the area form Company K of the Confederate 19th Tennessee Infantry; others later join C Company of the 63rd Tennessee Infantry, Confederate States of America (4).

After Tennessee joins the Confederacy, its state government attempts to control the Union-leaning eastern counties. At first it tries accepting the region's political views. After all, the East Tennessee Valley links Georgia and Virginia, creating a supply funnel that both sides will covet during the war. But Union sympathizers begin traveling northward through the valley to enlist with the Union in Kentucky. They often use the roads that pass through Bean Station, and many of them receive food, directions, and shelter from sympathetic East Tennesseans.

This supposed disloyalty upsets the state's Confederate leaders, and soon the inevitable happens. They dispatch a Confederate Army into East Tennessee to deal with the increasingly hostile area. So, of course, relations deteriorate even further. In November of 1861 the situation explodes when Unionists burn five key railroad bridges, limiting the amount of supplies and troops that can be transported through the Tennessee Valley. Confederate authorities retaliate by imprisoning several hundred men and by imposing martial law (5). East Tennesseans now truly grasp that they live in enemy territory. Martial law prevents local leaders and courts from making and enforcing policy; instead the Confederate military does so. For citizens such as the Harris families, this system of government means the end of their civil rights concerning searches, imprisonment, and freedom of movement. The public is at the mercy of the army.

As the Civil War continues, the news of 1862 establishes that America's conflict with itself will be an extensive one. Decisive victory proves elusive for either side, and several battles end disastrously for Union forces, including the battle of Fredericksburg. The Federals capture New Orleans, though, giving them partial access to the Mississippi River, another supply line. Because it needs men to fight, the Confederacy declares all white men between the ages of eighteen and thirty-five eligible to be drafted into its army. As residents of a Southern state, East Tennesseans are eligible for conscription whether they sympathize with the Confederacy or not. In fact, the draft often consists of Southern patrols simply encountering men and forcing them to enlist. This practice makes a precarious situation even worse for B.Y. and others, giving an element of danger to the briefest trip off the farm. Even though at thirty-six B.Y. legally surpasses the age covered by the conscription act, he is as vulnerable as his younger brothers to forced enlistment with the Confederacy.

As these events unfold, the Harris families continually assess the situation. Brother-in-law Almarine Wynkel argues the men should immediately sign up with the Union. The veteran glamorizes his exploits during the Mexican-American War, describing exotic lands and peoples. At age forty-four Almarine plans to fight again. Soon he will start recruiting for the Union Army in Grainger and nearby counties (6). But first he recruits among his wife's family. Almarine knows how much of an asset the five Harris brothers could be in battle. Certainly he doesn't want to fight against them.

Almarine Wynkel

But B.Y. doesn't believe they should enlist just yet, not with a Confederate Army in East Tennessee. The completion of a railroad through the Tennessee Valley diminished Bean Station's status as a transportation hub, but the town still intertwines with two prominent roads. Entire armies could march through the area, and the Harris brothers have property to protect. Plus B.Y. thinks constantly of Lucretia and his children. Unlike those in other regions of the country, his family can't outwait the war, worried but safe in Grainger County. Protecting them is his priority, and for that he must be at home.

Validation of this decision comes swiftly. One of the most disastrous features of the war, one that devastates civilian life, soon unfolds in East Tennessee. The Confederate Army undersupplies its troops in the region, so it begins feeding its soldiers through confiscation. In other words, the army forages, taking food for men and fodder for animals from the area's civilians. At first Confederate sympathizers willingly help; pro-Union ones less so. But as the war continues, troops demand more than food from the local population; they confiscate goods ranging from kindling to farm animals (7). Since the army takes supplies indiscriminately, all families sacrifice.

In fact, during the war's first year, Confederate foragers approach B.Y. and Lucretia's farm. Because of his tobacco business, the barn contains a huge amount of the crop belonging to himself, his extended family, and his neighbors. The loss of this tobacco would cause hardship across the community. When the looters arrive, B.Y. and nine-year-old son Will are mucking out the barn stalls. They hurriedly cover the tobacco with loose hay; then B.Y. rushes to be with Lucretia at the house. The foragers demand food and investigate the barn, but B.Y. convinces them that he already sold the tobacco. The valuable crop remains hidden under a layer of hay for the remainder of the war (8).

Similar confrontations with the Confederate Army, almost all of them ending with confiscations, cause increasing chaos for the region's farmers. After all, this raiding steals both food and livelihood from East Tennesseans. Martial law protects the army rather than civilians, so farmers have few rights. Because the army's foraging results in frustration and food shortages, and society's governing bodies have essentially collapsed, a crime wave begins in East Tennessee that outlasts the war (9). Criminal gangs from both sides of the conflict emerge to live by scavenging and profit from intimidation; Grainger County becomes immersed in turmoil, repeatedly reporting "violent theft" (10). In addition, the conflict looms nearby; Bean Station residents can hear brief military engagements from their homes (11). The Harris family's sense of prewar prosperity vanishes, as does their sense of security. B.Y.'s preoccupation with the price of tobacco or with crops being harvested morphs into fears of livestock stolen, the farm vandalized, his family harassed.

Thus the first two years of the Civil War pass with East Tennessee in constant turmoil. Most economic activity ends, and normal life proves elusive. With animals stolen and crops confiscated, civilians in this lush farming region experience fear and hunger. In contrast to their prewar prosperity, the Harrises and other Grainger County residents now just try to survive. But the area's distress and its loyalty to the Union haven't gone unnoticed. During the war's first years, President Lincoln himself pushes to have East Tennessee liberated from its Confederate occupiers (12). Finally, in 1863, a long-awaited decision occurs, and the Union begins raising an army to free East Tennessee from the Confederacy. Scores of local men enlist.

Unfortunately the Union's intent becomes widely known, so the Confederates busily conscript men to repel the coming invasion.

As for B.Y., his wheat crop proves his undoing (13). On the road home from the mill in Mooresburg, he encounters a Confederate patrol. He greets them courteously. A brief discussion ensues when they inform him that now is his time to enlist. B.Y. agrees to join their cause, promising to arrive at their camp as soon as he can gather weapon and clothing. He rushes home and hurriedly tells Lucretia about the confrontation. The dreaded moment of parting having arrived, they hug each other intensely. B.Y. kisses his children but must leave Lucretia to answer their tearful questions.

He hurriedly wraps a few belongings within the quilt that covers his and Lucretia's bed. For a moment he rests his hand on the carved headboard and closes his eyes, wrestling with the knowledge that he must leave his family at this terrible time. After all, Will is only nine, James five, and Louisa a toddler. Daily life teems with danger.

After a moment, B.Y. straightens, then picks up his gun and the quilt holding his possessions. Afraid the front door is being watched, he climbs out the bedroom window, scrambles over the back porch roof, and drops silently to the ground. He shivers in the chilly air but knows that soon the spring crops will need planting. Only no one will be on the farm to do it. Nevertheless, he steels his heart and heads directly toward Clinch Mountain and Kentucky…to join the Union Army (14).

CHAPTER 4

The 8ᵗʰ Regiment Volunteer Infantry of Tennessee, Company I

IN THE QUAGMIRE of conflict that exists in 1863 East Tennessee, motives for enlistment with the Union are many. In January U.S. President Lincoln announces the Emancipation Proclamation, a justly celebrated event which technically frees slaves in all areas of the U.S. currently in rebellion. But the reality differs. Tennessee is a Confederate state; however, it is exempted from the proclamation and its slaves not freed. For Union soldiers fighting to abolish slavery, this creates a bitter contradiction. Still, East Tennesseans enlist for reasons other than abolitionist viewpoints. Many believe in a United States and feel it should be preserved. More prosaically, the Confederate conscription act is hugely unpopular. This law destroys the population's ability to stay impartial and pushes citizens toward action (1). In addition, farmers fear the war's inevitable effect on their livelihoods. Since the Union army these East Tennesseans join has the express purpose of ridding the region of Confederates, many enlist to oppose the confiscation of their livestock and produce. Perhaps Joseph Bare, one of B.Y.'s friends and fellow soldiers, says it best. He expresses several concerns in a letter to his wife when he says of the Confederates, "I don't like for them to be on our Tennessee soil...the Union and Old Constitution is what I am after now" (2).

Whatever their reasons, in 1863 East Tennessee men enlist with the Union in droves.

In March when thirty-six-year-old B.Y. arrives at Camp Nelson, Kentucky, he is greeted by two of his brothers. William, his closest brother in age and friendship, enlisted in January, along with Richard, the youngest sibling (3). Plus, B.Y. doesn't arrive alone. On his way to Kentucky he stopped at his father-in-law's household to say good-bye and ask William Gray to watch over Lucretia and the children. When B.Y.'s brother Jim heard about his confrontation with the Confederates, he decided to enlist also (4). For the older brothers, joining the war effort means leaving their wives, children, and farms to the uncertainty of a violent era. Richard's enlistment brings complications too, even though he is twenty-two and unmarried. While growing up he was both loved and harassed by his brothers, who accused him of having an easy life as the youngest. Much as older brothers always feel about younger ones, B.Y. considers Richard considerably less hardened than himself but grudgingly feels responsible for him. Richard, of course, hates this attitude.

By midsummer oldest brother Thomas also enlists, and all of the Harris brothers but long-lost Booker are committed to the Union (5).

East Tennesseans overwhelmingly comprise the regiment that B.Y. and his brothers join, the 8th Tennessee Volunteer Infantry. Many of these men live in Grainger, Hawkins, and Greene Counties, which occupy much of the upper Tennessee Valley. Other family enlistees from the Bean Station area include brother-in-law Almarine Wynkel and David T. Harris, a first cousin whose family immigrated to Tennessee with B.Y.'s family. After several transfers during the summer, all these men, another Harris brother-in-law, and numerous neighbors congregate in the 8th Regiment, Company I, under Col. Reeve. Companies often contain men from a single neighborhood because their established camaraderie creates cohesive units. It also leaves the home community vulnerable to extensive loss. Other notable enlistees in the 8th Regiment include Stokley Gray, B.Y.'s brother-in-law, who is a corporal in G Company (6), and Joseph Bare, the letter-writer who grew up near the Grays and is in Company I with the Harris brothers (7). Thomas Bible from Greene County is captain of C Company and keeps a journal throughout much of the war, detailing the experiences of the 8th Tennessee. Other relatives and neighbors join the 4th Volunteer Tennessee Regiment, including two of B.Y.'s cousins and a brother-in-law (8).

Eventually, of David Harris' ten children in Tennessee, every son and every son-in-law enlists with the Union. Every one of them.

Having this many men in uniform naturally leaves a void back home. Now women and elderly men must feed families and contend with the occupying army. In fact, the Union's decision to liberate East Tennessee from the Confederacy causes a mid-war upheaval in the region's ongoing crisis. In Grainger and Hawkins Counties, David Harris, aged sixty-seven, and William Gray, aged seventy-five, must abandon the relative ease of old age and return to the role of family protectors. They strive to support their daughters, daughters-in-law, and grandchildren, but with four young families disrupted and four farms shorthanded, not every interest can be protected.

Once B.Y. joins the army, Lucretia's parents implore her to return to the relative safety of their Hawkins County home, but she insists on staying at her and B.Y.'s farm. Abandoning the property would leave it vulnerable to raiding and vandalism. Her daily routine changes drastically as she no longer indulges in fine clothing and town social activities. Days of relative leisure now behind her, she struggles to care for the horses, cows, and chickens while also keeping a garden. When not worrying about feeding her children, she fears for B.Y.'s health and safety. In fact, everyone experiences a gnawing and relentless apprehension, families for their sons and husbands at war... soldiers for their wives and children at home.

As the Harris brothers settle into army life at Camp Nelson, home of the 8th Tennessee, they soon experience its problematic conditions. The muddy, unsanitary camp breeds diseases. Within its confines the scourge of the war soon becomes apparent: diarrhea. Far from its modern reputation of causing humorous embarrassment, this disease kills untold Civil War soldiers on both sides of the conflict. In fact, during the war more men die because of disease than through the astronomical losses of battle. The many causes of diarrhea range from food poisoning to viruses, such as giardia, to parasites and bacteria, such as salmonella and E. coli (9). With so many men living in close proximity and latrines sometimes positioned upstream of the drinking supply, these organisms easily move from one gastrointestinal tract to another. If one of them travels beyond a soldier's stomach to his colon, the resulting disease is called "dysentery" and causes chronic problems that include diarrhea, vomiting, weight loss, and dehydration—ills that make the rigors of army life almost intolerable. Once contracted, dysentery proves difficult to overcome, and soon the soldier becomes thin and weak because of a lack of nutrients. So these illnesses are incredibly serious.

Throughout the war the 8th Regiment will lose fifty men in battle but two hundred and twenty-seven to disease (10). Unfortunately, the Harris brothers are not immune. By the time B.Y. and James arrive in camp, William already suffers from a serious case of diarrhea.

Camp conditions such as these are common, but more telling differences exist among Civil War regiments. For example, the 8th Tennessee Volunteer Regiment that the Harris brothers join isn't exactly a glory unit. Volunteers might be more highly valued than draftees, but they lack the skills of a regular army soldier. The 8th's first assignments consist of fatigue duty and building defenses in Kentucky (11). Soon it combines with other regiments into the 9th Corps under the command of Major General Ambrose Burnside. For his part, Burnside's reputation isn't a glorious one either. He commanded the Northern Army of the Potomac but was strenuously encouraged to resign that position after his army suffered a humiliating defeat at Fredericksburg, Virginia. Leading troops in Kentucky and Tennessee represents a demotion for him. Of course, the enormous and senseless loss of Federal soldiers at Fredericksburg isn't exactly inspiring for the men under his command.

Nevertheless, in August the 8th Tennessee Regiment begins its promised assignment and becomes part of the Union's campaign to free East Tennessee from the Confederates.

Burnside separates his army into several columns that take various routes from Kentucky into Tennessee. The 8th Regiment becomes part of Burnside's 2nd Brigade, which travels southward on the Cumberland Plateau, the mountainous barrier that separates the east and middle sections of the state. They traverse difficult terrain past the small towns of Wartburg and Huntsville. The roads are curved, hilly, and often washed out, notoriously problematic for transporting large groups of soldiers and the vast amounts of food and ammunition they require. Partly because of the resulting supply problem, the troops are almost immediately placed on half rations (12). Even while poorly fed, Burnside's army manages to cross the mountains, and the various columns convene in Loudon, Tennessee, in the midst of the Tennessee Valley, southwest of Knoxville.

By early September when the troops reach this destination, chronic diarrhea has so weakened William Harris that he can no longer fulfill his army duties. He enters a hospital at nearby Lenoir's Station (13). Soon he will return to Hawkins County to recuperate at home. This pattern recurs countless times throughout the war for soldiers in both armies. Once recovered, most return to the fight.

Meanwhile William's brothers serve with Burnside's army in the Tennessee Valley, trying to protect the Chattanooga-to-Bristol railroad, the one that runs up the Tennessee Valley and facilitates the movement of troops and supplies. In reality the Federals only operate within the valley's center section between Loudon, where the Confederates burned a railroad bridge, and Greenville, quarters for six thousand of the enemy (14). These two armies don't fight wide-scale battles, but they do engage in numerous small scrimmages.

Except for living on half rations, this is army life as B.Y. anticipated it, with regulations to follow, hours of drills, and a fair number of card games. But he yearns for a decisive battle against the Confederates. If the Union gained control of East Tennessee, his family would be safer. Such a victory wouldn't mean that he could go home, though. All the soldiers enlisted for a three-year term.

Soon the men begin writing their loved ones. B.Y. and Lucretia have known one member of the company, Joseph Bare, for most of their lives. In fact, Joseph grew up next to the Grays (15). He writes to his wife, Elizabeth, clearly aware that the letter's contents will be shared with others. In fact, he addresses it to "wife and friends" and includes information meant for specific community members. Individual soldiers are mentioned, including Richard Harris. Like all the men, Joseph worries about his farm, although he is clearly respectful of Elizabeth's abilities. He tells her to harvest the wheat crop and to "manage what little is thare to the best advantage for I think you are a prity good manager" (16).

Trying not to worry his wife, Joseph speaks lightly of the war: "Our forces and the Rebs are skirmishing once and a while but not much damage done...I understand that you are all very uneasy thinking the Rebs will come there, but I don't think there is any danger... I am in hope that their time is prity well round up" (17). Joseph asks about his son's health and assures Elizabeth that, except for a cold, he is healthy. He repeatedly implores her to write and have friends and family do the same.

By the summer of 1863, about the time that Burnside's army enters Tennessee, the American Civil War has been raging for over two years. The conflict is finally beginning to appear winnable for the Union, mainly because of the surrender of Vicksburg on the Mississippi River and the defeat of Confederate General Lee's army at Gettysburg, Pennsylvania. But to the people of the era, much uncertainty remains. The Confederacy decides it can still win the conflict by not quitting with the goal of eventually exhausting the Union's resolve. Then, the theory goes, United States politicians will compromise to achieve peace. This strategy depends on several factors, including two military feats which will allow the Confederacy to function while losing territory. Two areas must remain in its hands: Richmond, Virginia, because it is the Confederate capital, and Atlanta because it is an important supply hub (18).

Naturally taking these two cities becomes a priority for the Federals, but doing so won't be easy. Even after its defeat at Gettysburg, Lee's army aptly protects the Confederate capital. Also the Federals must first take Chattanooga in the lower Tennessee Valley in order to open a road toward Atlanta. That effort recently received a setback when a Union army was defeated at Chickamauga, Georgia.

To win the war this way, the Confederacy also needs the Union's population to lose commitment to the war effort. Civilians on both sides know incredibly large numbers of men are dying, and not just from disease. Civil War battles are shockingly brutal and becoming more so. There are casualty rates of over fifty thousand men at Gettysburg and almost thirty-five thousand at Chickamauga. Entire cities worth of men perish at each battle. Of course these horrors affect both sides. The Confederate 63rd Tennessee Infantry, containing men from Mooresburg, takes part in the battle for Chickamauga and loses almost half of its troops. Even victories devastate in this war.

Back in East Tennessee, Burnside's army facilitates the quest for Atlanta by engaging the Confederates, hoping to gain control of the Tennessee Valley. This goal would be more attainable if the Union soldiers were well fed. Instead they exist on half rations because the region's mountainous terrain continues to disrupt the army's supply system. In reality that system was never feasibly planned. About a month after the army enters Tennessee, the order is given for the ranks to begin foraging (19). The Confederate Army has been confiscating food and supplies from civilians for two years, causing great suffering for civilians. Now the Union one joins it.

The Federal Army orders this foraging out of desperation, and many of its leaders are sympathetic to the decision's inevitable effect on locals. One commander, General Granger, states that "nothing has pained me so much as being compelled to strip the country; friend and foe must fare alike, or the army must starve" (20). This Federal general tries to mitigate his army's effect on the local population by restricting confiscation. He gives "the most stringent orders… to prevent marauding," but acknowledges that "hungry men are difficult to control after fasting for five months on half and quarter rations" (21).

The command to forage for food appalls the Harris men. They signed up to free East Tennessee from Confederate rule and now must prey on the very communities they intended to help. As landowners and farmers themselves, they understand the devastation that the Federal Army's foraging will bring. Plus the order endangers their families at home. Far from being looters and thieves, they are substantial people, the type of citizen whom the army will be looting from.

But, of course the Harris brothers will forage for food. That's the reality of war.

CHAPTER 5

Battling Longstreet

SADLY, THE FEDERAL Army's invasion of East Tennessee makes life even more dangerous for the region's civilians. The local skirmishes and small-arms fire that the area first experienced are now joined by large-scale battles fought in small towns and major cities. Before the war ends, the two voracious armies will conduct extended campaigns that twice take them almost the entire length of the Tennessee Valley and back (1). The armies' constant movements throw the region into turmoil, with communities especially disrupted when occupied by one side and then the other. For example, when Confederates command a town, they sometimes mistreat its Union supporters. Once the Federal Army gains control, those Unionists often retaliate against the Southern sympathizers who earlier harassed them. With so many sons and fathers in uniform, emotions run high, and both sides succumb to violence and vindictiveness. In fact, hostage-taking joins confiscation of goods and arrest as a means of retaliation for both Union and Confederate sympathizers (2). In short, all civility disintegrates.

Once it controls territory in East Tennessee, the Union Army emulates the Confederates and declares martial law. The Federals create the office of the Provost Marshal General to administer this law and appoint General Samuel Carter to the job. Carter manages thirty-two deputy provost marshals who often oversee their home regions in East Tennessee. But these deputies aren't always reputable or evenhanded and they sometimes contribute to local controversies. Instead of providing a consistent governing force, many use their positions for retaliation and other abuses. This, of course, contributes to the region's general lawlessness (3).

Living in Grainger County amid such issues, Lucretia struggles to work the farm, especially while caring for three children age ten and younger. Will's childhood crumbles as he toils beside his mother, but he, too, must work for the family to survive. These two can keep a garden and feed the livestock, but they cannot feasibly plant large fields of crops. They also struggle to make repairs to fencing and outbuildings, chores which are invariably increasing. The family has gone from wealth and comfort to want and insecurity. Lucretia knows her family's food is vulnerable to confiscation, so she hides everything she can, including the preserved meat. The building where B.Y.

processed tobacco has a loft which is only accessible by a side ladder, and she hides the salted ham there, under some corn fodder.

Soon enough foragers from the Union Army ride into the yard. Lucretia experiences real fear when the soldiers demand food. While the toddler Louisa screams in her arms, Lucretia hands over the family's corn meal and lard. Will and Tommy watch helplessly, knowing those items would have provided cornbread for their supper. Meanwhile two soldiers search the farm for hidden food or possessions. One man climbs the ladder and looks in the tobacco loft but doesn't shift far enough through the fodder to find the ham. Thus the pork is saved, at least for the time being (4).

Lucretia was lucky. Just as General Grainger predicted, the Federal Army turns out to be at least as destructive in its foraging as the Confederate one. For his part, Provost Carter tries to deter this plundering of civilians. He formally complains to the army's chief of staff about conduct by army foragers, charging that in "a widely prevalent evil…horses, forage, provisions, and not infrequently household effects are taken by wholly unauthorized persons, leaving no receipt or voucher of any sort… Robbery, theft, fraud, and open outrageous violation of all law seems to characterize their conduct in every part of the country" (5). Carter then requests that these renegade actions be punished and that more stringent guidelines be issued on confiscations, but it does no good. Such thievery on the part of Union troops continues.

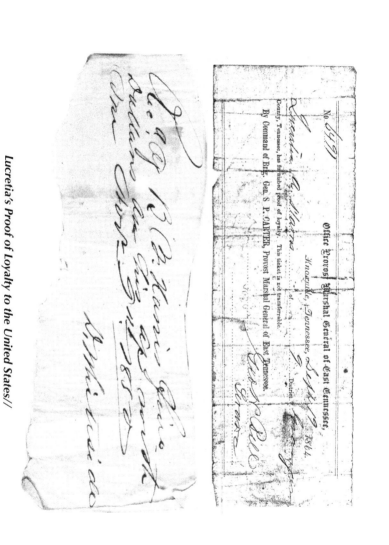

Lucretia's Proof of Loyalty to the United States;//
B. Y.'s receipt for payment on his bar tab at the Bean Station Tavern

Ironically, while Lucretia struggles to outwit marauders and manage a farm, her husband and other members of the 8th Volunteer Tennessee Regiment languish with inaction. They do accompany Burnside's Union troops when the city of Knoxville surrenders after a brief struggle (6). The city greets the army as liberators, or at least its Unionist sympathizers do. Unfortunately, Knoxville has divided loyalties: 51 percent of its population voted against secession and 49 percent for it (7). No matter who is in control of the city, half the civilians experience the fear and abuse of living under occupation.

The bulk of Burnside's forces soon leave Knoxville and move southwest through the Tennessee Valley to engage the Confederates. The 8th Regiment, however, receives orders to help hold the city (8). Camped just south of Knoxville, east of the Cherokee cliffs that overlook the Tennessee River, they have a fine view of town and sections of the adjoining countryside (9). But they grumble at being left behind, and morale suffers. Why keep endlessly drilling, they wonder, if they are not going to fight?

Burnside's forces soon begin a running battle with General James Longstreet's Confederate Army. The two engage at Huff's Ferry outside of Loudon and then at various points up the Tennessee Valley to Knoxville. Once Burnside returns to the city, the army commandeers homes and cuts down trees to use in the town's defense. The troops hurriedly strengthen the city's defenses, burning houses and businesses, and erecting solid, chest-high barriers, called "breast-works," along several main thoroughfares. In mid-November General Longstreet tries to retake Knoxville with a brief, rather ineffectual, siege. The technique fails, partly because East Tennessee loyalists send food downriver to town. Finally Longstreet orders an assault against the city's weakest point, Fort Sanders, which sits on top of a ridge and has dirt fortifications. The 8th Tennessee Volunteers are still camped on a nearby ridge top during this short but intense battle for the city, but they don't take part. In truth their assistance isn't needed: The Federals win a decisive victory. Only about twenty Federals die compared to six times that many of the enemy. In addition Union troops wound over four hundred Confederates and capture over two hundred. The conflict does devastate Knoxville, vandalizing the formerly attractive city with combat and occupation (10).

Once he loses the battle for Knoxville, Confederate General Longstreet leads his army northward into upper East Tennessee. Four thousand Union cavalry and infantrymen chase after them, but to the Harris brothers' chagrin, the 8th Regiment is again left in Knoxville. On December 14th Longstreet turns to face his pursuers.

He does so in Bean Station.

Similar to Knoxville's experience, the small town is transformed as an army prepares for battle. The

Federals reach Bean Station several days before the Confederates, and during that time thousands of soldiers prepare for war by building breastworks similar to those erected in Knoxville. Confederate General Longstreet's plan of battle is to trap the Federals in town. His forces arrive from the north, and he sends troops to cut off the other routes, including the western road over Clinch Mountain. An intense battle ensues in the center of town that rages for hours. Well over a hundred Federals position themselves in the old tavern because it contains several stories and faces multiple directions. Citizens huddle in their homes' cellars or back rooms, deafened by the sounds of massive gunfire and soldiers' cries of encouragement and agony.

The battle rages all day, but eventually the Confederate troops begin to prevail. One of their last missions is to overcome the Federal forces inside the frontier-era Whiteside Inn. Large guns are used on the tavern as the Confederates fire at it from three sides; its brick construction is punctured and shells detonate inside (11). Many Union soldiers die there. Once it becomes clear that the battle is lost, the Federal Army retreats toward Knoxville. While doing so they set fires west of the tavern in order to confuse the enemy (12). Between the two sides, 1,600 soldiers are either killed or wounded in Bean Station. Longstreet's Confederates also soon move on, crossing the river to establish winter quarters about thirteen miles away.

The next day Bean Station citizens must contend with the aftermath of battle. Most of the Federal dead were removed by their army, but many Confederate bodies are left behind, creating a graphic picture of war at its most grotesque. Left to bury hundreds of men, the townspeople quickly inter most of them in the town cemetery. But this is only the first step toward cleaning up. In their quest to prepare for battle, the armies vandalized, burned, and destroyed. They also left behind the waste of thousands of men in close quarters.

Upon learning of this battle, B.Y. and his brothers worry intensely about their families. Their farms are a few miles outside of town, within easy reach of both armies. Also, a Confederate victory so close to Bean Station is unnerving to everyone. When he hears details of the confrontation, B.Y. contemplates the business he has conducted at the old tavern and the many enjoyable times he spent there with his friends and brothers. With the building now marked by blood, war has forever altered another part of his life.

Back in Knoxville the regiment that was withheld from these battles soon comes under formal criticism. An inspection report states that "the 4th and 8th Tennessee Regiments… (are) in bad condition as regards appearance, discipline and drill" (13). These are the very two regiments which contain Grainger and Hawkins County volunteers. Reasons for the problems are many. First, the army isn't providing enough food, clothing, or footwear for these soldiers (14). The army's failure to oversee foraging inevitably weakens discipline. In addition, regiments comprised of citizen soldiers are not highly regarded by the army, no matter how immersed the men and their families are in the conflict. For their part, the Harris brothers are frustrated with their regiment's idleness, especially when the war invades their hometown. Thomas rages against this forced inaction and frequents Knoxville's taverns. B.Y. and Jim understand his anger but instead concentrate on reminding the captain that his men just want to fight. Richard has been on several detached missions and finds his role in war more satisfying than the others, but he, too, is impatient.

᠑᠑᠑᠊

The battle of Bean Station marks the beginning of a devastating winter for East Tennessee. In the upper valley, Longstreet's Confederates camp about fifteen miles outside B.Y.'s hometown. This army forages so heavily that it decimates the area (15). Meanwhile the Union Army lives off the land around Knoxville. When no food remains to forage, civilians and soldiers in both locations suffer. These burdens overwhelm the once-prosperous region. A Confederate officer sympathizes that "East Tennessee is bleeding at every pore...literally eaten up" while a Union one comments that the two armies leave "extreme destitution...among the people" (16). Other combatants celebrate this chaos. One Confederate major leads a foray into Hawkins and Hancock Counties, then brags of acquiring several strong horses and striking "terror into the whole country" (17).

Finally in late winter Federal troops begin traveling up the Tennessee Valley to engage the enemy (18). The Harris brothers gladly leave Knoxville with their regiment, which is now part of Major General John Schofield's XXIII Army Corps. For the next several months the Confederate and Union Armies again vie for control of East Tennessee, skirmishing from Knoxville to Morristown and points in between.

But war and deprivation demand a toll.

Though they are relieved to be fighting, the men of Company I suffer from the ghastly winter. Having left Knoxville, they face the elements with insufficient food and clothing. B.Y. appreciates the quilt he brought from home and is glad he had the foresight to carry it all summer. By February many men are ill, including Joseph Bare, who wrote his wife about life in Company I. Joseph assured her that he was well except for a bad cold, but a winter of hunger and tent-living have severely weakened him. In fact when illness renders him unable to keep up with the Federal troops, he is left behind and soon captured by the enemy. The Confederates take Bare to Virginia and admit him to a hospital in Richmond. But Joseph's illness has progressed too far, and he dies there on February 16th (19). His earlier letter to his wife Elizabeth contained a poignant good-bye: "If I never see you any more I shall never forget what you said to me the other morning… if we never see each other on earth I want to meet you in heaven, where parting will be no more" (20).

Joseph's death is a cruel blow to Elizabeth and their young son, but it also affects the Gray sisters, especially Lucretia and Margaret. They are friends with the couple, attended their wedding, and realize all too well that, being in the same regiment and company, their husbands endure the exact circumstances as Joseph.

In the midst of these broader events, there is a personal tragedy within the Harris family. Since the war's beginning, Almarine Wynkel has recruited for the 8th Tennessee Regiment in Grainger and Hawkins Counties. William Harris, B.Y.'s brother, has been assisting him, having somewhat recuperated from the illness that forced him to leave the regiment. Recruiting raises their profile in the community, however, and in January a Confederate patrol ambushes and captures them. The thought of William and Almarine in a Southern prison disturbs both their families. William's parents and wife Mary especially worry about his health. A prison is no place to recover from dysentery.

Unfortunately East Tennessee's winter of destruction and pain does not result in a clear outcome. Most soldiers and citizens endure. No one wins. In April, Confederate General Longstreet and his army leave

Tennessee for Virginia, and there is a brief period of inactivity for the Federal troops. The XXIII Corps is reorganized and the 8th Regiment placed in Colonel Reeve's Brigade. B.Y.'s younger brother Jim is promoted to first sergeant of Company I under Captain Graham (21). Even better, the regiment is close to its soldiers' homes, and for four glorious days, they are granted furlough (22). The men gladly walk the miles to Bean Station. After all, they have not seen their families in over a year.

When B.Y. arrives home, Lucretia and the older children are shocked at how much he has changed. Thin and dirty, he barely resembles the handsome man of business who Lucretia married. Son Will notes how appallingly fragile his father looks. Lucretia teases her husband for taking the quilt from their bed when he left so abruptly to enlist. Rips and filth now cover the previously beautiful blanket, and she vows privately to attempt repairs during his few days at home. For his part, the state of the farm disheartens B.Y., but he tries to hide his despair from Lucretia and Will. He hears details on the Battle of Bean Station and how the Confederates captured William and Almarine. B.Y. visits his parents and his father-in-law, trying to help when possible. Soldier and civilians carefully assess each other, wondering how the others are really holding up behind their assurances. In reality everyone is simply enduring, gritting out the war.

On April 8th, after the four-day break, Jim and Richard return to the regiment while B.Y. and his brother Thomas report in sick (23). Certainly they have health to regain after a year of army life, and Thomas in particular is suffering from the chronic diarrhea common among the ranks. But the brothers planned this action. While at home, B.Y. and Thomas plant spring crops for their own families and for their father. B.Y. also does what he can for William Gray and for Mary, his brother William's wife. Soldiers within both armies sometimes take these self-appointed furloughs as they attempt to serve their cause while also ensuring their families don't starve. By July, with crops in the ground, B.Y. and Thomas return to their regiment (24). This takes some doing on their part, because by then the 8th Tennessee is in Georgia, embroiled in one of the war's major campaigns.

CHAPTER 6

The Thick of War: Atlanta

BY THE SPRING of 1864 both sides are tired of war, including the Confederates, who are not winning major battles, and Unionists, who never expected such horrible loss of lives. Both sides have similar death rates; almost 24 percent of soldiers die from battle and disease (1). Bureaucracy, even for the Union, is unprepared for and overwhelmed by this number. In the best of circumstances officials record sporadic information before burial, but no formal process exists to notify relatives of a death. Thus, both sides know that hundreds of thousands of men are dying, but it proves almost impossible to find out if a relative is one of them. In the North the issue is so serious that a political party arises which proposes ending the war.

If the Confederate strategy of winning by not losing appears viable, it soon develops a weakness. General Lee's army still protects Richmond, Virginia, but the Federals force the Confederates from the Chattanooga, Tennessee, area in November of 1863, opening the road to Atlanta. From this railroad hub in north Georgia, supplies are sent throughout the South. Taking it would seriously disrupt the Confederate cause, but Union troops must fight their way to the city. Both sides send additional forces to this important war zone, although the Union has an advantage with a larger population to recruit and draft from. The Federals also have units that can undertake more direct roles in battle. Thus, in May of 1864, the 23rd Corps, which includes the 8th Tennessee, receives orders to move south into Georgia to help General Sherman's army take Atlanta from Confederate General John Hood.

In this way B.Y.'s regiment moves beyond its stated purpose of freeing East Tennessee from Confederate hands and joins the larger theatre of war.

During the spring and summer of 1863, the 8th Regiment battles relentlessly at Allatoona, Marietta, Buckhead, and Peach Tree Creek (2). The men are under heavy fire at the Battle of Resacca on May 14th and win a bloody exchange the next day. For the next several weeks their activity alternates between skirmishing, some of it heavy, and marching as the army slowly but relentlessly makes its way southward. In June, the 8th Tennessee spends a week guarding an ammunition train, and at Kenesaw Mountain, Captain Bible's C Company functions as sharpshooters in the front of the action. By early July, crops in the ground and health regained, B.Y. and Thomas rejoin their regiment. Such absences are common, and their comrades, especially Jim and Richard, are pleased to see them. The older brothers find the 8th Tennessee already changed since it was left behind at Knoxville. The constant fighting has hardened the men into a combat-ready regiment.

B.Y. and Thomas Harris leave a region also moving into another phase of war. When the Union and Confederate Armies depart from East Tennessee, abbreviated forces remain behind, but a power vacuum still forms. Deserters and criminals with little or no allegiance to either side of the conflict exploit the area's lawlessness, causing increased crime and destruction (3).

Of course, both sides blame these problems on the opposition. When a lawless gang preys on a Union family, Confederates receive blame for the atrocity, but when that same gang preys on a Confederate family, the Federals are condemned. In Knoxville Unionist instigator and newspaperman Parson Brownlow vehemently denounces area Confederates and encourages Unionists to violence. Thus the two groups of civilians constantly demonize each other. In June Grainger County makes a formal request to form a National Guard company for its protection (4). Unfortunately, the so-called Home Guard sometimes become lawless gangs themselves who prey indiscriminately on the population. In the resulting chaos, many families simply leave East Tennessee, moving north out of the war zone as refugees, while those who stay face a reality of hunger and crime (5).

East Tennessee Provost Marshal General Carter knows the region is under siege. He writes another letter to the Federal Army, formally complaining about the behavior of its mounted forces in East Tennessee. Carter states:

> It is well known that the farmers in the major part of East Tennessee have been robbed of their stock to such an extent that they have not one-half enough left with which to cultivate their lands… that soldiers are in the habit of taking horses and mules wherever they can find them, and of disposing them for their own benefit. As men who are guilty of such acts have but one object, that of gain, they, of course, rob a Union citizen with as little hesitancy as they would a rebel sympathizer. …The force which has just returned from upper East Tennessee brought with it a number of mules and horses altogether too young for service (6).

In other words confiscations are being made for personal profit instead of to benefit the army. With this letter, Carter again tries to stop the raiding of civilians, but some of his actions are more controversial. For example, he orders that East Tennesseans be required to take an oath of loyalty to the United States. When Lucretia is asked to sign this oath she does so, thinking of the sacrifices she has made for her country, and of her husband and brother, who are risking death in the United States forces. At this point the war's demands appear endless.

❧❧❧

In mid-July the 8th Tennessee fights its way with the rest of General Sherman's Union army to within eleven miles of Atlanta as the struggle for this major Southern city intensifies. For B.Y.'s regiment, the conflict is most costly at the Battle of Utoy Creek on August 6th. General Sherman wants to secure a rail crossroads which is behind the enemy line, so he orders that a Confederate position be charged. The battle is crucially delayed because of a power struggle when a third Union general refuses to take commands from General Schofield of the XXIII Corps (7). Schofield's men, including the Harris brothers, must linger for a day near the battle site while the squabble is resolved by Sherman. Meanwhile the Confederates furiously fortify their position. When the battle occurs on August 6th, much of the action centers around Union General Reilly's brigade, which includes the 8th Tennessee. When the 8th Regiment attacks, it almost immediately begins to suffer heavy losses among officers and enlisted men. In his journal Captain Bible of

C Company describes warfare as B.Y. and his brothers experience it:

> "We were in an open field, protected only by the uneven ground. Plungling (sic) shot screaming shell, grape and canister, swept overhead and around us which hideously rent the air; the earth trembled and the Heavens appeared like a blaze of fiery hail... My Company was enveloped in fire, shots, and shells; truly in the vally (sic) of Death, held in the hollow of God's hand" (8).

During this intense battle, Reilly's Brigade twice charges the Confederate line. Amid the smoke, gunfire, and screams, the Grainger County men plunge toward the enemy with primal intensity. The 8th Regiment comes closest to the enemy than any other regiment in the brigade; furthermore, amid real carnage, its men fight until ordered to retreat (9). The soldiers then entrench, but never reach the railroad line as ordered.

After the battle, the Union's senior officers unanimously praise the 8th Tennessee. Regiment Commander Berry says that "the officers and men of the regiment exhibited in the highest degree the bravery, discipline, presence of mind which characterizes veteran troops" (10). Brigadier General Reilly officially notes "the gallant and heroic conduct of the

Eighth Tennessee Infantry officers and men, without any distinction. The list of casualties, however, is their best eulogy, when it is known that the regiment went into the charge with but about 160 muskets" (11). As the general admits, some soldiers were not even fully armed during the battle. Clearly, men of the 8th Tennessee Regiment who were denounced as unruly in Knoxville comported themselves with more discipline than the generals at Utoy Creek. But it hardly matters.

This battle devastates the Harris brothers.

Twenty-four-year-old Richard, B.Y.'s youngest sibling, dies in combat, bleeding to death as the battle rages around him (12). Sergeant Jim Harris is shot in the face and falls to the ground screaming while blood pours over his features. Although B.Y. and Thomas see their brothers writhing on the battlefield, they must ignore them while charging as ordered.

After the battle ends, the army also reports Jim as dead (13). In fact, a fourth of the regiment dies, is seriously wounded, or taken prisoner at Utoy Creek (14). Of the two men dead and five captured from Company I, B.Y. has known them all since childhood. The day's carnage and their personal losses overwhelm B.Y. and Thomas. Weary, filthy, and half deaf from the cannon fire, B.Y. numbly contemplates Richard and Jim's deaths. Now Richard will never hunt game in the Rocky Mountains, will never marry, or see home again. Amid his stunned despair, he dreads writing his parents. The only greater pain than Richard's death would be informing his mother of it. And Jim. Margaret will be inconsolable upon learning of her husband's death, and Lucretia will grieve with her sister.

Soon, however, B.Y. and Thomas receive miraculous news. Jim is alive! Four days after the army reported him dead, it discovers him living, housed in a Georgia hospital and suffering from a serious infection. Eventually his head wound heals to a small scar beside his eye, but more serious effects linger from Jim's battlefield experience. In mid-September he briefly tries to rejoin the regiment, but being left for dead and losing Richard render him incapable of returning to the fight. Soon the army removes him from the combat zone, and from mid-October through the spring he stays in the Deaf and Dumb Asylum Hospital at Knoxville, suffering from diarrhea, dysentery, and "chronic rheumatism" (15). At this point, no mention is made of his original wound. Jim finds healing difficult with hundreds of men crammed in the makeshift hospital and overflowing into tents on the hospital yard. Even detached from the war, he struggles with guilt and despair.

Back in the ranks, Company I and the rest of the 8th Tennessee attempt to forget the crushing losses of Utoy Creek. B.Y. and Thomas grimly realize that of the five brothers who volunteered to fight, only they remain.

CHAPTER 7

Middle Tennessee

THE WAR RAGES on, unfazed by mishaps like Utoy Creek. Finally in early September Atlanta falls, and the conflict's endgame begins to play out. Confederate General Hood leads his defeated army away from the city into Alabama. For his part Federal General Sherman divides his forces, sending the 23rd Corps, 8th Tennessee Regiment included, after Hood's army. By pursuing the Confederates, the brothers are saved from being part of Sherman's terrorizing march from Atlanta to the coast. Sherman demoralizes citizens by confiscating and destroying their food, deliberately leaving them desolate in the face of winter (1). The general does order that homes and barns only be burned when civilians resist his troops. But since those troops are systematically plundering stored food, resistance occurs.

The 8th Regiment of Tennessee, however, serves more honorably under the command of Major General

John Schofield. They chase Hood's army from Georgia into Alabama and then Middle Tennessee. After several months of skirmishing, it becomes apparent that the two armies will soon fight a major battle. The catalyst occurs one night when Hood's forces allow Schofield's divided and vulnerable Union Army to slip by them (2). The Federals actually pass within sight of the Confederate campfires (3), and once past Hood, they reunite and regain full strength. This lost opportunity infuriates Hood, who sends his army in pursuit.

Around daylight of November 30th Schofield's Union forces arrive first into the small town of Franklin. They must remain there until a destroyed bridge can be rebuilt. The troops sleep for an hour, then work frantically to reinforce their position with breastworks in case the Confederates arrive before the bridge is complete. Schofield doesn't particularly want to fight in Franklin, thinking that he would have more of an advantage in Nashville, but Hood pushes the issue. The Confederate commander's controversial decision to fight in Franklin sets up the "bloodiest five hours of the war" (4). Troop numbers between the two forces are fairly even, but in order to meet their opposition, the Confederate forces must cross open fields, then overcome several tiers of breastworks that reach almost eight feet high.

At around four o'clock that evening, notes Bible, "the Great and Bloody battle of Franklin was begun" (5). The Confederates advance and break the forward

Union force fairly quickly but then meet more serious opposition. The main Union line is the one reinforced with chest-high breastworks that provide cover for artillery and riflemen. When the first Confederate brigade reaches this line, its men simply vanish in seconds, churned into the chaos of war (6). Right behind this unfortunate group: the 19th Confederate Tennessee Infantry. Men from Mooresburg, Tennessee, across the county line from Bean Station, comprise almost all of its K Company (7). Of course the 19th suffers horrendously high casualties. The Union's main line is eventually breeched, and the battle rages with barbaric results. Finally a Union brigade led by Col. Opdyche initiates a violent exchange and stops the barrage of Confederates. Opdyche's men are just the first reinforcements who enter the battle. The 8th Tennessee, with its two hundred men, reinforces the main line just west of Opdyche's brigade (8). Thus B.Y. and Thomas again fight in the midst of an onslaught. For five hours the action is relentless.

Captain Bible describes the contribution of the 8th Regiment of Tennessee at Franklin. When the enemy surges forward, the regiment is:

> immediately ordered to advance…which was obeyed. Then came the awful struggle. One volley and then another; then rose the war cry and the clasp of arms rose higher… The earth seemed to reel rock and tremble and the

ground strewn with wounded, dead and dying. The Sun hid his face in the smoke of battle
until he sank below the horizon and left the
awful scene in darkness (9).

B.Y. and Thomas abhor this savagery, but feel
lucky to survive. At Franklin the brutality of mankind
becomes staggeringly apparent, even among many
such gruesome Civil War events. But at least the regiment's losses don't equal those of Utoy Creek. The
Confederates, however, suffer a devastating loss with
six thousand casualties among the ranks and six generals dead.

As the battle of Franklin illuminates, regiments
from the Grainger/Hawkins County area are fighting
for both sides of the war. They participate in heavy
fighting and sustain serious losses, sometimes while
battling each other. Afterward these soldiers will return to their communities in East Tennessee. Many
will harbor hatred and resentment. No one will forget. The lofty ideals that often compelled them to war
disintegrate before this trauma. Bitterness, anger, and
resentment will be the reality.

The Middle Tennessee showdown between
Confederate and Union Armies culminates within
weeks. After the battle of Franklin, the Union Army
leaves the town as soon as possible, around midnight.
In twenty-four hours the soldiers have snuck past
Hood's troops in the dark, slept for an hour, fortified

their position, fought one of the war's bloodiest battles, and now are marching away. Inexplicably Hood orders his severely beaten army to follow them. A few weeks later in December, the two armies clash at Nashville. On the first day of battle, the XXIII Corps acts as reserves. In particular, the 13th U.S. Colored Infantry relieves the 8th Regiment and participates in the battle for their freedom (10). The next day the 8th Tennessee storms the hill containing Redoubt #5, taking four pieces of artillery and capturing two to three hundred prisoners (11). This feat enables Shy's Hill to be taken and helps determine the day's outcome. For the Federals, the battle of Nashville provides a decisive victory.

If taking Atlanta was one of the two criteria needed for the Union to win the war, not only has Atlanta fallen, but the army that protected it is decimated. Soon General Sherman finishes his march through Georgia and writes President Lincoln, gifting him with the city of Savannah as a Christmas present. Only Virginia and North Carolina remain in Confederate control.

But the men who actually make these victories possible are struggling. Worn from illness and frequent marching, mental rather than physical strength propels them through the last lonely months of the war. B.Y. hardly dares contemplate that he might return to his family and the hills of Grainger County.

In early 1865 as the American Civil War winds down, the 8th Tennessee is sent eastward into North Carolina. To get there they travel the Tennessee River by steamboat, then march, ride trains, and even sail past Mt. Vernon to the Atlantic Ocean (12). Bible, whose native Green County sits across the Tennessee Valley from Grainger County and is easily as hilly, has spent years recording his wartime experiences in East Tennessee without ever complaining about mountainous terrain. However, with the regiment aboard ship, a February storm vastly impresses him: "At Sea," he writes. "Rain! Storm! Waves running very high! Anchor until the storm abates" (13). Bible and the other East Tennesseans navigate mountains and foothills with ease, but the vast and foreign ocean intimidates them. Soon the regiment disembarks from the ship and marches through North Carolina from Wilmington to Kingston. This six-day trek leads them through "quicksands, swamps, and lagoons" (14). Even though the Union will clearly win the war, for B.Y. the last days of conflict provide a quagmire of misery.

On April 9th Confederate General Lee finally surrenders his army at Appomattox, Virginia, and the Civil War effectively ends. Five days later all celebrations abruptly end when President Lincoln is assassinated. Uncertainly reigns throughout the country.

After several more weeks, on June 30, 1865, the army pays and discharges the men of the 8th Volunteer Regiment of Tennessee. Finally B.Y.'s enlistment ends.

The soldiers ride the train from North Carolina to Nashville, decorating it with the company colors and celebrating the Fourth of July along the way with crowds of well-wishers (15). In horrible irony, though, Thomas Harris' chronic diarrhea becomes debilitating. For the past year he has periodically visited one army hospital after another but always managed to stay with the regiment. Now, on his way home, with the war over, he enters a Nashville hospital (16). The remaining men of the 8th Tennessee travel by rail to Knoxville, which is as far as the railroad lines devastated by war can take them. So from that point, B.Y. and the surviving men from Grainger and Hawkins Counties tiredly begin walking home.

CHAPTER 8

Andersonville Prison

NO CIVIL WAR prison camp possesses a good reputation. Virtually all captives suffer from hunger, disease, and despair. But the unbelievably horrid conditions of the Union and Confederate prisons evolve gradually throughout the war. Early in the struggle, prisoner exchanges occur after each battle, which makes camp conditions bearable because the men are captive for relatively short periods of time. This practice becomes problematic, though, because most men almost immediately return to the fight. When the exchanges end by the summer of 1863, many temporary holding pens become permanent facilities. The resulting overcrowding intensifies issues such as the spread of disease and the inability of guards to guarantee the prisoners' safety. Southern prisons especially grapple with the latter problem because their guards are often old men and young boys (1). As within the Confederate and Union Armies, insufficient rations are common, again especially in the South, which late in the war faces increasing food shortages.

But individual prisons on both sides of the conflict hold specific horrors. At Belle Island, Virginia's facility, Federal prisoners suffer from a smallpox outbreak. In Elmira, New York, scores of Confederate captives freeze to death when provided too few stoves for the winter of 1865. Of over twelve thousand prisoners in Elmira, almost 25 percent die of sickness and exposure (2).

But the Confederacy's Andersonville, Georgia, prison prevails as the worst facility for several reasons. One is its sheer number of captives, in total around 45,000 men. Out of desperate need, the camp opens when still incomplete, with its housing facilities unbuilt. By May of 1864 it holds 12,000 men, with five hundred more arriving each day. These prisoners receive severely limited rations and must fear each other in the crowded and inadequately guarded camp. A notorious band called "The Raiders" rob, terrorize, and even murder their fellow prisoners. Even with these issues, Andersonville's main problems stem from lack of sanitation. The stream used for water runs through camp and is also used for hygiene purposes. It becomes contaminated soon after the camp opens. Thus the war's endemic problems, diarrhea and dysentery, cause the vast number of casualties. These men perish from weight loss and dehydration; in essence they starve to death. Combine this with inadequate shelter and rations, and the scene horrifies.

In total 13,000 of the prisoners will die.

The conditions appall even Andersonville's Confederate officials, so they repeatedly ask the Confederate government for more money and more food for the prisoners. Camp Commander Captain Wirz writes a Colonel Chandler, noting that he hopes "your official report will make such an impression with the authorities at Richmond that they will issue the necessary orders to enable us to get what we so badly need" (3). In the trauma of an increasingly lost war, the Confederate government barely responds. Eventually camp officials capture and hang the murderous gang of prisoners, but the situation still worsens. Several captives keep journals and mail service provides some contact with the outside world, spreading word of the camp's environment. The prisoners themselves sign a petition describing the conditions and asking to be exchanged. This document reaches the Federal government in Washington, but no reply ever comes.

Because of the terrible reputation of all Civil War prison camps, the Harris families despair in January of 1864 when Confederates capture William Harris and Almarine Wynkel. The men were recruiting for the Union, a dangerous enterprise in East Tennessee. Also, Almarine had recently drawn attention to himself by playing the Confederate authorities for fools. When he and his group of Union recruits met a Confederate patrol on a Grainger County road, he jovially handed over his "Confederate" recruits, then rode off (4). When the real Confederate officers woke the next morning to discover that most of their new men had vanished overnight, they quickly grasped Almarine's ploy.

This audacity makes Almarine an intensely wanted man, so he begins recruiting for a new company in the 8th Tennessee Regiment which he will captain. He, William, and several others meet in Hawkins County at the Bishops, neighbors of David Harris who also support the Union. The men leave their guns at the door in order to enjoy a meal, but Confederates soon surround the house and retrieve the weapons. Without their guns to resist, the men must surrender or be killed (5). News of their capture spreads quickly, but their families have no knowledge of their whereabouts. The Confederates transport Almarine to Bell Island, Virginia Prison Camp but soon release him because of poor health. He spends close to six months recuperating in a Nashville hospital, then goes home (6). To recruit again.

Unfortunately, the Confederates send the others, including William and a Mr. McAnally, to Andersonville (7). Upon entering the camp's walls, the men realize that its awful reputation is not exaggerated. The prison's crowded and desperate inhabitants emit a palpable stench that makes the new captives reel. The prisoners' faces reflect anguish and despair, and the Grainger County men instinctively know they must collaborate just to survive. They jostle for a small plot of land, then scavenge and pay for odd bits of lumber and tin in order to construct a lean-to. Within days they are infested with lice. Then the diarrhea begins.

For over a year they suffer greatly while enduring the overwhelmed prison at its worst. Having just spent months recovering from a life-threatening case of diarrhea, William is particularly vulnerable. He becomes desperately sick and fights to survive until the war ends. He often daydreams of his wife Mary and marvels how a man who just wanted to farm could end up in this horror. Finally camp authorities tell many of the camp's prisoners, the Grainger County men included, that they can relocate to a better facility nearby. William insists on moving with his comrades, even though in his weakened condition they advise him not to try. He falls behind during the march, and they lose track of him (8).

By 1865 when the war ends, the Andersonville camp is being used as a prison hospital, full of men dying of chronic diarrhea and dysentery. Soon photographs of these prisoners join the descriptions of camp life circulating in the Northern press. The emaciated, dying soldiers become symbols of the camp's shortcomings, furthering assumptions that they were deliberately starved. In the turbulent times after Lincoln's death, an outraged public demands retribution, especially of Captain Wirz who oversaw the camp. His official pleas for more food and money unacknowledged, he is quickly tried and executed for his actions as camp commander. In July no less than Clara Barton attempts to identify the graves of men buried at Andersonville.

None of this helps Private William Harris, who dies of chronic diarrhea around June 9th, probably while alone and surrounded by filth and degradation (9). He leaves behind a young wife and three daughters, ages eight, five, and three (10). Family members are never notified of his death. Over a hundred years later, his grand-niece, Gladys Winkles Shaver, will tell his story with such fervor that her voice shakes. While in her eighties, she visits the Andersonville Prison Historical Site and finally confirms William's fate. Taking a photograph of gravesite number 1766, she mourns a relative who she never met.

Roughly 620,000 Union and Confederate soldiers die during the American Civil War. Even more men survive their service but experience private agonies stemming from years of bloodshed and loss. In addition, during the conflict countless women and children endure direct contact with brutality and deprivation. It's a lot to overcome.

CHAPTER 9

Aftermath

AS THEY WALK home during the summer of 1865, B.Y. and the other men traverse a landscape ravaged by years of war. The road conditions between Knoxville and Bean Station rival that of the destroyed railway. Four years of overuse by men, wagons, and animals have left a heavy legacy of deep gouges competing with exposed rock. As the veterans leave Knox County behind them and enter Grainger County, damaged fences and barns continually mark the roadside farms. Summer brought growth and greenery, but these farmers recognize an abundance of weeds among the scattered fields of crops. Overly thin locals scan the men's faces with interest, searching for a loved one. At this point in their journey, both citizens and veterans numbly turn away. The leg broken as a teenager pains B.Y. constantly. He wonders how his brothers are doing, who is alive and who dead. He contemplates the fate of his wife, children, and parents. He limps toward home.

In upper East Tennessee most Harris family members do initially survive the war, including B.Y.'s wife, Lucretia, his parents, and his brother's wives and children. These civilians must wait anxiously for weeks and even months for the soldiers to return. Because the Harris brothers begin journeying home from different locations, they arrive home separately. In late June the army discharges Jim from its hospital in Knoxville (1). About the same time that he starts toward Bean Station, Thomas enters the hospital in Nashville where he will spend months recovering from illness. Then he, too, must walk part of the way home.

Still, endurance is often rewarded, and one remarkable summer day B.Y. and Lucretia finally reunite. They hold tightly to each other for long moments, standing unsteadily on the porch of their home while their children watch in exhaustion and trepidation. She is appalled at how dirty he is but laughs at the filth-encrusted quilt he still carries. He smiles wryly; returning it comprised a small victory. Such wonderful news as B.Y.'s return quickly spreads to his parents and other families waiting for soldiers and prisoners. Homecomings spawn joyous celebrations; everyone is elated at the war's end.

Only the war doesn't end for East Tennessee and Grainger County.

Years of hunger, crime, and turmoil have taken root. Neighboring households that supported opposite sides during the conflict now contain veterans from those opposing sides, men such as B.Y. and Thomas, who watched a brother die. Even worse, other families grieve for soldiers who perished during the war's horrific battles. Veterans of both armies hear their families tell stories of life during the war, stories featuring stolen property, threatened wives, hungry children. Perhaps inevitably, the wartime violence persists. In January of 1866 a Union veteran and neighbor to David Harris is killed in Hawkins County in front of three witnesses. His tombstone bluntly reads: "murdered at Rogersville" (2). His family gets revenge, though, since the man charged with the homicide doesn't survive to stand trial (3). Certainly Unionists aren't the only targets. Many postwar acts of retaliation occur against Confederates, including the ambush and assault of two men in Grainger County (4). Even after four years of conflict, it's unclear whether postwar East Tennessee will be led by Unionists or by former Confederates; therefore, murder, thievery, assault, and retaliatory abuse of the legal system continue for several years (5).

The strain caused by the war and its long denouement of crime and bitterness appears immediately in the Harris family and in ways that gradually evolve. All the veterans experience uncertain health, with Jim and Thomas especially affected. At age thirty-nine B.Y.

must rebuild his life, but he finds serious challenges at home. Lucretia's health suffered during the strenuous war years, and she spends much time resting. Their eleven-year-old son Will can help farm, but he, his eight-year-old brother Tommy, and five-year-old sister Louisa have gone years without a father's presence in a time of lawlessness and fear. Will angrily lashes out at B.Y.; Tommy hovers underfoot, while Louisa hides. B.Y. senses they all need reassurance from him, but such intangibles become lost amid more pressing concerns.

In fact, B.Y. most worries about feeding his family through the winter. He arrives home in late summer, too late to plant most crops. The army paid him mustering-out money for his years of fighting, but the amount doesn't compensate for his absence and the war's destruction. He could use the pay to help feed his family through the winter and purchase materials to repair the farm, but the money wouldn't stretch far enough to also buy seed for the spring crops (6). B.Y. desperately needs cash, and he still owns one somewhat valuable possession: land. In October he and his father sell mineral rights to some of their property, twelve hundred acres for David and almost two hundred for B.Y. (7). If any commodities such as oil, coal, and salt are discovered there within the next fifty years, the mineral will be mined, with the company earning ninety percent of the profit and the Harrises ten. David and B.Y.'s gamble could ruin their land; mining practices of the era often destroy acreage downhill or downstream from the mine. However, Grainger County's section of the Cumberland Mountains contains no coal, and the mineral rights are never executed. Even more importantly, two families survive the winter.

B.Y. does return home to some encouraging news. The tobacco which he hid from looters early in the war still rests securely under a pile of hay in the barn. He takes it to market in Danville, Virginia, and, after consulting his carefully kept records, distributes the proceeds amongst the crop's growers or their survivors. In the postwar environment, this tobacco brings more than any other crop he ever sells. The entire community profits.

Apart from such fortunate events, the war's toll on civilians soon becomes apparent. Lucretia's seventy-eight-year-old father, William Gray, has difficulty adjusting to the many setbacks which occur so late in his life. He dies in 1866, and B.Y. is appointed executor of his estate (8). Gray's demise isn't unexpected, but with three of his daughters married to three of the Harris sons, it reverberates throughout the families. Even though his holdings lost value during the war, the women inherit a significant amount of money from their father. B.Y. and Lucretia use it to make repairs to their farm. Margaret gains the family home where she and Jim have been living since they first married, making him head of a household which includes their three children as well as her widowed mother and sister (9).

Mary's inheritance helps her to care for her and William's children. But she struggles in his absence. McAnally and the other recruits who were captured with William eventually return from Andersonville Prison. They hoped to find him at home, but after learning he is still missing must report what they know from last seeing him. He is probably dead, but they can't be sure. The well-publicized horrors of Andersonville torment Mary, who can't make herself stop reading accounts of the prison, hoping illogically to glean some news of her husband. She and her children, B.Y., and his parents wait fruitlessly for William's return, overwhelmed by the ambiguity of not knowing his fate. Thousands of other men also disappear into this war-induced turmoil, seized by enormous forces that leave no trace of them. For Mary and many other East Tennesseans such heartaches allow the pain of war to strengthen its grip and hold relentlessly.

Unfortunately William's continuing absence and Gray's death aren't the Harrises' only postwar tragedies. Soon after returning home, B.Y. must face a bitter truth: Lucretia, his wife of fourteen years, has consumption. Stress and poor nutrition triggered the infection she contracted when nursing her own mother during the disease's last stages. Lucretia grows progressively thinner and weaker. As her health declines, she experiences sweating and chills, and coughs so horribly that her body shakes and her lungs produce frothy blood. People of her era know that the disease flourishes among families and assume that it is inherited. Consumption actually threatens entire households by spreading through the air.

B.Y. struggles with the unfairness of his wife's illness. Lucretia labored so valiantly during the war years to protect their children and farm, never dwelling on her vastly reduced circumstances. Now with his return, instead of her situation improving, she is dying. He wishes that her life had been easier and regrets that he couldn't make it so. Her relentless disease soon prevails, and a little over a year after B.Y.'s return, after much suffering, Lucretia Gray Harris dies at age thirty-nine (10). On a bleak November day her husband, three children, and surviving family members bury her in the Lebow family cemetery.

Lucretia's death delivers the blow to B.Y. that even the war couldn't, as he mourns her and their lost future. Since the war, he has focused on providing for his family and labored valiantly to do so. But a few weeks after her death, he turns forty and numbly wonders if starting over is feasible at his age. Amid the pain of Lucretia's death his customary resolve eludes him. First he loses momentum and then purpose. Regrets take their place, and his actions during combat begin to haunt him. He remembers too well the sounds of clashing armies, the confiscation of goods from hungry civilians, the random atrocities. The grimace of death. Wrestling with his own actions, he wonders in despair if killing during war is considered murder. As these thoughts merge and simmer, a bizarrely raging numbness settles over him. He starts depending on his parents to help raise his children and frequents Bean Station's taverns instead of staying home.

Months pass, then a year, as B.Y. struggles with grief and rage.

Of course B.Y. isn't the only veteran to suffer. Every East Tennessee soldier leaves the brutality of war and returns to its legacy of crime and division. The radical Unionist Parson Brownlow is now Tennessee's governor, and he actively encourages his supporters to retaliate against former Confederates. Chaos rules East Tennessee, not calm in which former soldiers can re-acclimate to society. In an era with no concept of mental health, some veterans never recover and simply live in turmoil.

All three Harris brothers feel the effects of their time in uniform. Thomas' health fails to improve, and he remains chillingly silent. Jim endures long-term issues from his head wound and has memory lapses. As the veterans and their families suffer, it soon becomes apparent that all East Tennesseans, in fact all Americans, must make a crucial choice: perpetuate the bitterness of war or attempt the difficult task of forgiveness and rebuilding.

For B.Y. and his extended family, a lifeline comes unexpectedly. John and Elizabeth Brooks are neighbors of David and Polly whose son dies soon after the war's end. Even though Mr. Brooks is not a religious man, he and his wife feel the need to grieve with their community and decide to hold a memorial service. No pastor lives nearby, but Mr. Brooks has briefly met a Reverend Molsbee in Rogersville, so he invites this pastor to conduct the service (11).

Molsbee happens to be a member of the Church of the Brethren, a denomination that originated centuries earlier in Germany. The Brethren follow the once-controversial idea that baptism should occur when one is old enough to consciously choose salvation. Similar to the Mennonites, they were persecuted in Europe for this belief, so by the early eighteenth century they began moving to the American colonies in large numbers. The Brethren also believe in the guidance of Jesus and follow the New Testament. They adhere to a third core belief, this time one similar to the Quakers. The Brethren are pacifists. They admire the intent of Ephesians chapter four, verses one through three: "Beseech you that ye walk worthy of the vocation wherewith ye are called, with all lowliness and meekness, with longsuffering, forbearing one another in love; endeavoring to keep the unity of the Spirit in the bond of peace" (12). To the Brethren, war and human aggression form the crux of human ills.

This belief in peace permeates Reverend Molsbee's sermon and resonates within his audience of veterans and their families. After all, not only does the aftermath of war reverberate within them, but they are being encouraged to sustain its conflict. The reverend presents a powerful alternative. The Harrises soon reject Governor Brownlow's calls for continued violence and choose peace instead. Reverend Molsbee preaches in the community several more times, and eventually ten families, including the Harrises, Barrs, Meeks, Brooks, Campbells, Isenbergs, and Longs, organize a church (13). These founding members include David and Polly Harris, William's wife Mary, and Jim and his wife Margaret. Furthermore David's daughters are married into the Long and Meek families, and the Barrs are the family of Joseph Bare, whom B.Y. fought with in Company I of the 8th Tennessee Regiment. In short, the entire community establishes this new church.

Never a particularly religious individual, B.Y. strongly feels the need to atone for his time at war, for the senselessness at Utoy Creek and Franklin, where he knows his actions ensured that other men died. Also, he hates the aimlessness that has gripped him since Lucretia's death. Seeking a sense of renewal, he donates land for the congregation's first church (14). In this time of deprivation the members build a simple log cabin to house the Meadow Branch Church of the Brethren. B.Y. and his father David are made deacons, and Jim serves as the congregation's first minister (15). Within this church the community gradually replaces feelings of bitterness and loss with those of peace and renewal. Meetings occur several times a month and include rituals such as the repast, which commemorates the last supper of Christ, and baptism, which involves immersing an individual three times backward. This congregation and its beliefs become guideposts that help B.Y. again find meaning in life. He tries to come to terms with his actions during the war and attempts to accept Lucretia's death. Achieving such goals, though, will be a long-term endeavor.

CHAPTER **10**

Perseverance

A YEAR LATER in December of 1868, B.Y. experiences one of life's milestones when his father dies (1). David Harris lived almost seventy-three years, fighting in the War of 1812 and bringing his family westward into prosperity. He taught his sons farming and mentored them into adulthood. During his burial in Long Cemetery on the south side of Clinch Mountain, B.Y. stands stoically by his mother as they grieve with David's many children and grandchildren. David's will provides for Polly, but she soon moves in with her daughter Elizabeth, leaving the farm and all its contents to be sold.

Polly and daughters Mary and Susan purchase most of the household items, including two cupboards and bedsteads, a mirror, a clock, a set of Staffordshire china dogs, and two books, one of which is the early nineteenth-century best-seller *Life of Washington* (2).

When the farm goods are dispensed of, Mary buys a yearling, Thomas ten sheep, and B.Y. practical items such as a horse collar, brace and bit, mattock and tobacco cutter. Jim only purchases a book on medicine. After their move to Tennessee in a covered wagon, David and Polly established a household of grace and comfort, and as the farm is readied to sell, all the children are saddened by this further break with their prewar lives. B.Y. has always valued this lush, productive farm and particularly dislikes the thought of it leaving the family.

In fact, David's passing provides a catalyst for B.Y. Lucretia's death rendered him uncharacteristically passive for over two years and triggered anguish over his wartime actions. Now, he finally acknowledges that all their prewar lives are lost, vanished into the same abyss as William. If he doesn't act, the family homestead will be lost too. B.Y. can purchase most of the farm, but he needs help running it. Sadly after the war there are many available women in the Bean Station area, many of them widows.

But B.Y. has strong feelings for his sister-in-law Mary.

They have known each other since childhood and often socialized as in-laws. In the four years since the war's end, B.Y. has helped Mary with chores and tried to be a father figure for his nieces. As William's wife and brother, the two talked long hours about his kindness and strength, the probability of his living.

In contrast to Lucretia, Mary can read and thus more closely equals B.Y. in education (3). After caring for her children during the years without a husband, she has become independent and strong. Vastly changed from the young woman who thought she couldn't begin married life without a servant, Mary's thoughtful and resourceful personality complements B.Y.'s ambition. Mainly, when with Mary, B.Y. feels desire again, but the improbable possibility that William might still live haunts him. How would he and Mary explain themselves if his brother returned?

Nevertheless, in March of 1869, B.Y. weds Mary Gray Harris, his brother's widow and sister to his own dead wife (4).

The ceremony takes place at the couple's new farm, recently purchased from David Harris' estate. The groom's brother Jim officiates. The small gathering includes family and church members who bring food and good wishes to the party. They all comment on how well Mary looks, how this marriage lifts the weight of war and loss that she bore for so long. She encouraged her husband to buy David's farm for several reasons, some of them nostalgic. The land belonged to her Lebow grandparents and she fondly remembers playing there as a child. In fact, the site and farm are surprisingly intact this soon after the war. The fertile land and wooded ridges will help the couple reestablish themselves.

Thus when a new decade begins in 1870, forty-three-year-old B.Y. owns a farm with proven potential and has again married out of love. He might now be more of a sustenance farmer than before the war, but at least he provides for his own. His household bustles with children. His son Will is now sixteen, Tommy twelve, and daughter Mary Louisa ten. Of Mary and William's girls, Sarah is twelve, Catherine ten, and Rebecca eight. All the children attend school, and everyone in the family but Louisa can read (5).

Having learned harsh lessons during the war, B.Y. and Mary begin a series of legal maneuvers designed to protect their family. B.Y. becomes legal guardian of Mary and William's girls when he, their uncle Stokely Gray, and David Harris' estate all provide five hundred dollars to each child (6). For years B.Y. carefully accounts for the girls' finances, adding the pension received for William's war service and periodically deducting costs for schooling, clothing, and special events (7). Most of the money stays in trust so the girls will have means when they come of age. The same three men also pledge $300 to B.Y.'s children, and he becomes guardian of their inheritances also (8). As always he keeps careful records, filing numerous court reports over the years, and storing paperwork in a wooden document box that sits near the front door of his home.

Just as B.Y. and Mary strive for stability, so does East Tennessee. But chaos and desolation prevailed there for years and don't easily dissipate. The region continues to exist in a quagmire of conflict. Amid this postwar chaos, it gradually becomes apparent that East Tennessee will keep its close Union ties. With this issue settled, citizens plan for the future, and Confederate sympathizers voluntarily relocate or are forced out of the region. Bean Station's situation is typical as the exodus results in a loss of workers ranging from laborers to artisans. Because of this dislocation and the number of war dead, society itself experiences instability as it tries to readjust.

The amount of ruined infrastructure exacts a toll too, especially in the destroyed railroad that once facilitated the region's antebellum economic boom. Even Bean Station's famous tavern falls on hard times, so the courts order that it be sold. An ad in the Knoxville paper admits that the building was "the scene of a battle, all of which resulted in some spoliation and waste…The large and elegant brick hotel, one of the largest, best constructed and most costly structures in East Tennessee can be easily repaired" (9). In reality the property suffers from the destruction and death that occurred during the battle of Bean Station. It and several other prominent town properties totaling over three hundred acres are sold at auction in a time of economic disarray.

This exodus of ex-Confederates leaves East Tennessee with an overwhelmingly Union-leaning, Republican-voting citizenship. By 1870, however, Parson Brownlow no longer governs the state, and soon the Democratic party popular in the western and middle regions regains the governorship. Mostly veterans and supporters of the Confederacy, these

Democrats have little sympathy for the eastern counties with their divisive war legacy. Also, only Virginia endured more Civil War battles than Tennessee, so the state needs to rebuild everywhere. For years East Tennesseans will feel that the state government focuses on the middle and west regions to the detriment of their own eastern counties.

Problems like this repress the already hurting region. In particular, farmers, the heart of the East Tennessee economy, are devastated by the war. In the decade between 1860 and 1870 their wealth falls by 39 percent, which means the real losses caused by the war are higher but offset by gains made between the war's end and the decade's end (10). Such a drastic reduction in wealth also reflects the loss of two-fifths of the area's farm animals (11). B.Y. isn't at all immune. From 1860 to 1870 the value of his farm plummets from $2,300 to only $1,000 (12). For years he lacks the capital to replace the farm animals lost to theft and conscription. This loss of wealth also reflects lower real estate prices and land he sells at repressed values in order to survive. Recovering economically from the war will be a long process for all East Tennessee farmers.

Across the region Southern Unionists know they endured much of the brunt of war. In contrast, northern states were the site of few major battles and even enjoyed a strong economy during the conflict (13). After the war ends, East Tennesseans and other Union supporters who lived in the war zone complain vigorously about the food, livestock, and household goods confiscated from them by Federal troops. Finally, the U.S. Congress creates the Southern Claims Commission to consider repayment for goods taken from loyal Unionists by the Federal army. But with over four thousand claims submitted by Tennesseans alone, the commission leaves itself many loopholes. It specifies, for example, that payment will only be made for legal, not illegal, foraging (14). East Tennesseans know that line was crossed repeatedly and almost as soon as the Union Army entered the region. Since it was widely documented that the Federals couldn't control the foraging of their own troops, Tennesseans find this restriction completely unfair.

One of the many claims submitted to the commission is filed on behalf of William Gray's estate. Two witnesses report that the 100th Ohio wagon master confiscated a black horse from Gray without making payment (15). Gray's son Stokley and three sons-in-law fought for the Union, but the commission ignores such loyalty. In fact, the commission ignores reality when it officially considers all East Tennesseans to have been disloyal to the Union (16). The commission dismisses Gray's well-documented assertion of loss, along with the vast majority of claims it receives. Thus in a stinging rebuke to a loyal population who suffered so horribly to support their country, most farmers remain uncompensated for the Federal Army's extensive foraging.

J.T. (Tommy) Harris

Clearly East Tennessee must recover from the war on its own. A promising development occurs when the long-running crime wave diminishes and then officially ends around 1870. Even gradual improvements such as this one aid in rebuilding, and some citizens adapt to the new realities. B.Y.'s naturally entrepreneurial tendencies stir when he notices so many travelers passing through Bean Station in the postwar migration. With the railroad demolished by war, these migrants again follow the old roads. He hires a smith, provides the man with a home, and opens a blacksmith shop in town (17). After all, horses must always be shod and wagons must still be prepped to tackle Clinch Mountain. B.Y. keeps a ledger of all shop transactions with careful notations of the horse's name and owner, what hoof was worked on, and the fee charged.

More personally, B.Y. and wife Mary attempt to forge a new life together regardless of economics and state politics. When Mary realizes she is pregnant, both parents eagerly await their first child together. On June 10, 1871 the blessed event occurs, and Mary Harris gives birth to a son (18). She and B.Y. name him Jacob and proudly contemplate the joy of new life.

But their happiness soon proves to be sadly precarious. Childbirth kills more nineteenth-century women than any other cause and is especially devastating when combined with consumption. Mary came in contact with the disease when Lucretia did, as they nursed their own dying mother. Similar to her sister,

Mary's illness intensifies after a time of physical stress, in this case pregnancy and childbirth. As B.Y. watches with a terrible sense of helplessness, her health rapidly declines. She lingers for several months while desperately being tended by her daughters and women from the church.

Mary Gray Harris dies in September of 1871 after only two and a half years of marriage to B.Y. (19). Mother or aunt to all six children in the household, her loss devastates the family. Tragically, after his mother's death, the infant Jacob suffers too because a wet nurse can't be found for him. Women from the church frantically help B.Y. and the children care for him, but three more grim months end horribly when the baby dies just days before Christmas.

The six years since the war's end have been almost unrelentingly difficult for B.Y. He despairs over Mary's death and mourns deeply for her, who he knew for decades and risked the wrath of a beloved brother in order to marry. Jacob, a tangible sign of renewal, is mourned also. William and Mary's daughters, who are now orphans, grieve inconsolably. B.Y. wraps the girls in his arms and assures them a home throughout their lifetimes, should they wish it. All six children need this reassurance, having been traumatized by years of uncertainty and destruction. B.Y. deeply feels the immense responsibilities of fatherhood to a half-dozen children. Honed by hardship and war into a practical man, a survivor, he knows

life will move forward whether he wants to participate or not.

Therefore, a month after Jacob's death, a scarce
four months after the death of his wife Mary, B.Y.
Harris remarries.

CHAPTER 11

Yet Again

MARTHA BARR WAS just a girl of thirteen when the blue-eyed B.Y. left for war. Daughter of Peter and Betsie Barr, her parents live next to the Grays. She and her family worship at Meadow Branch Church with B.Y. and his children. Joseph Bare, who wrote his wife about life in the 8th Tennessee Regiment, Company I, was Martha's older brother (1). In truth Martha has many siblings and half-siblings whom her father sired over a long lifetime. Martha's mother married Peter when he was much older than she. Plus, as a teenager Martha romanticized the community gossip when B.Y. and Mary confronted their feelings for each other, then married in the face of William's possible return. Falling in love with her brother's comrade in arms is romantic too. Like William, Joseph never returned from a Southern prison, giving Martha and B.Y. a common tragedy. Lastly, she and several other women helped nurse the dying Mary and her doomed infant during their months-long illnesses.

At twenty-one Martha is of marriageable age, but a substantial twenty-four-year gap exists between her and B.Y. The war decimated the number of available men, and many veterans are amputees or suffer from health issues which hinder their ability to provide for a family by farming. These hard truths limit Martha's options. B.Y.'s reputation as a decent and industrious man strengthens his suit. As for B.Y., he desperately needs a wife to run his household and care for his children. They wed on January 28, 1872 in Grainger County at their pastor's house, and Martha enters a household deeply in mourning (2). Her first years there require patience and determination as the children adjust to her.

But life prevails, and a little over a year after Martha and B.Y. marry, she gives birth to their first child, John. Thankfully the occasion is uneventful, and both child and mother thrive.

So B.Y.'s household finally experiences good health, but his extended family still suffers from the war's effects. His war-time comrades, former brother-in-law Stokley Gray and cousin David T., are struggling financially. Also, his brother Jim hasn't recovered from nearly dying in the battle for Atlanta. Jim's wife Margaret has given birth once since the war, a son named James who was born a full five years after his father's return (3). Even though Jim must provide for a large family and keep up the Gray estate, he isn't bankrupt. Many men owe him money, but with the regional economy languishing and its communities in disarray, few can repay him. In a gut-wrenching decision these three men choose to leave Tennessee with their families and become part of a great migration of disenfranchised veterans.

In 1873 Jim and Margaret move to Missouri (4) along with David T. and his family. As children these men emigrated together with their parents from Virginia to Tennessee; later they both fought in Company I of the 8th Tennessee Regiment. Their close ties will help these families withstand the stresses of migration and resettlement. For his part, Stokley Gray moves to the open farmland of Kansas. B.Y. helps them all by purchasing David's land, collecting debts owed to Jim, and handling financial details for Stokley.

If B.Y. wants a change, a move with these men, particularly Jim, would be ideal. No other person dares to call him "Barty" and tease him like his only surviving younger brother. But B.Y. has buried two wives and two children in Tennessee; he lives on a productive farm that contains timber, pasture for cattle and sheep, and fertile acres for cultivation. While he hasn't completely recovered from the war years, he can provide for his family. B.Y. makes his choice and aligns his future with that of East Tennessee, staying in Grainger County and settling into marriage with Martha.

B.Y. and family. All have last name Harris unless otherwise noted. From left, back row: Prob. three children of Louisa Harris Gammon, Yancy, Ida Isenberg Harris, Porter, Brutus Winkels, Grace Harris Winkels, Ora Winkels. Middle row: Prob. Rebecca and Catherine, J.T. (Tommy), William (Will), B.Y., Sallie. Front row: two unknowns, Elsie Winkels, Gladys Winkels.

The trip westward and the years immediately afterward strain the three families. Stokley's health suffers, and when he is only sixty-six he enters a home for disabled soldiers in Kansas. Margaret dies during childbirth a few years after she and Jim leave Tennessee. She was the last of the three Gray sisters who married three Harris brothers in the prosperous antebellum years. David's wife Sarah doesn't survive long either. By 1880 he lives with his youngest sons and nine-year-old granddaughter. They are Jim's neighbors.

ﻮﻮﻮﻮ

Back in Grainger and Hawkins Counties, other community members feel more optimistic about the economy than Jim and David. A new railroad line connects Bean Station to Morristown, a small city about ten miles away. Similar to before the war, this railway allows area farmers easier access to regional markets. Also some non-farming jobs exist in the region. In Mooresburg men work long, taxing days at the salt mines and marble quarries, but they at least have jobs. At a mineral spring outside of Bean Station, Samuel Tate buys 2,500 acres and builds a hotel that can house five hundred guests. Medical opinion of the era considers mountain air to be helpful in fighting consumption, enabling many such establishments. Tate has grand ideas, and in advertisements targeted to veterans and their wives, claims the spring water cures chronic diarrhea and dysentery; liver, kidney, and skin problems;

and "diseases peculiar to females" (5).

The enterprise isn't without its setbacks, though. A cholera outbreak occurs during the summer of '74, killing a young woman at the hotel and sending guests scurrying. The epidemic spreads throughout the region, causing several more deaths. Tate eventually sells this first establishment to a Captain Tomlinson and buys a rival business, Mineral Hill Springs Hotel. He again advertises, this time flamboyantly touting the resort's scenery: "the Bean Station valley is one of the most beautiful spots in the world... From the lofty Clinch ...the myriad intervening hills appearing like broken waves of a vast ocean in tempestuous agitation" (6). For his part Tomlinson builds an ornate gazebo over the mineral springs on his property and envisions an elaborate Victorian resort, but such an ambitious plan will need time to unfold.

Businesses such as these greatly benefit the area economy. Tate employs what locals he can, then advertises in the Knoxville paper for two cooks and multiple hotel servants. He also needs a cooper to make a thousand barrels in order to ship spring water to customers who can't visit the resort. With all these workers newly in town, a cobbler and a physician set up practices in Bean Station, and a new hotel, stable, and general merchandising store open.

But economic hurdles still exist, partly because of war-time infrastructure damage. The old roads are in disrepair, with one section from the Holston River to Bean Station and another across Clinch Mountain almost impassable. The county doesn't have funds for repairs, so it sets a toll for use of the mountain road. This incenses the local citizenry who flood newspapers with letters to the editor vilifying the charge. In addition, Bean Station has developed a disreputable image, especially in the Skinflint and Clinch areas. The frontier-era taverns have degenerated into saloons that cater to drifters and teamsters, disenfranchised veterans, and even outlaws such as Jesse James (7). Public drunkenness and fighting become common enough to offend many townspeople. Even worse, the violence isn't limited to fistfights. Within a two-year period both a U.S. mail carrier and a U.S. marshal are murdered near Bean Station (8). Clearly the demise of the war-induced crime wave is uneven at best.

As for B.Y., he no longer finds the taverns attractive. Determined to adhere to his church's beliefs and regain his prewar prosperity, he concentrates on more productive pastimes. Certainly his household thrives with the energy of nine children. His three oldest offspring, Lucretia's children, live there with his brother William's three girls. He adores these nieces as beloved members of the family, sisters to his daughter Louisa. When the oldest niece, Sarah, turns sixteen, the family celebrates the event, and she excitedly spends sixty dollars of her inheritance on a horse. In addition B.Y. hires various tutors throughout the 1870s to educate Sarah, her sisters, and the majority of his biological children (9). Only Louisa never learns to read.

At this time, B.Y. and Martha have two offspring: two-year-old John and an infant, Porter. The baby inherited a skin disease from his mother's side of the family that frequently flares up. The scabs are uncomfortable and sometimes unsightly, but he is otherwise healthy. Much as he feels for his son's pain, B.Y. celebrates the successful birth.

In the way of farm families throughout time, all but these youngest members must contribute to the household. In general the boys help with the livestock and crops while the older girls assist Martha in the home and with the younger children. But life provides enjoyment too. When the circus is in town, the entire family attends, admiring the exotic animals, well-trained horses, and daring female acrobat. In fact, at least two thousand people see the circus in Bean Station, and all consider it one of the greatest amusements in the county since before the war.

As the decade progresses, B.Y.'s oldest children embark on independent lives. His niece Sarah marries on Christmas Eve of 1876 in a ceremony at his house. His oldest son Will also marries and begins farming nearby. Will preaches in the Brethren church and develops strong views on God's wrath. He insists that women dress plainly and restrict themselves to homemaking. The boy whose childhood was crushed by war becomes a harsh man.

Many young, local couples struggle economically, partly due to one of East Tennessee's land inheritance patterns. The area's early settlers snubbed the European concept of the oldest son inheriting a father's entire property. Instead, they divided their farms among all their children, girls included. After being inherited this way for generations, these enormous tracts of land have shrunk into parcels unable to sustain the era's large families. Some landowners do try to counteract the problem. Both John Lebow and David Harris ordered their land sold and the proceeds distributed among their children. Of course, in both cases, family members promptly bought the land back. Because of this practice, B.Y. could essentially purchase Lebow's entire homestead. But after the war many farmers trying to live on small farms must also tenant-farm for a landlord. This restricts their financial prospects because someone else claims their work's true profits. However, an inherently American solution exists to the problem: westward immigration to regions with cheap, plentiful land.

Will and Sarah's families choose the latter and soon move to Missouri, settling near B.Y.'s brother Jim (10). In contrast, son Tommy requires a push to leave home. At dusk on his twenty-first birthday, with a bit of fanfare, B.Y. remarks that his second son was born at sundown and presents him with a horse and saddle, the family's traditional gift for a man of his age. He then suggests that Tommy support himself by finding work as a hired hand. Tommy soon marries a local girl who inherits nearby land containing a large house. Later, he and a second wife open a school there.

By 1880, after almost fifteen years, B.Y. has finally recovered financially from the war's effects. At this time the average farm in Grainger, Green, and Johnson Counties contains thirty-eight acres, but he owns two hundred acres of pasture and farmland alone, putting him in the top 3½ percent of landowners (11). This much acreage allows him to prosper because he can rest fields between plantings. He also owns a hundred and thirty-five acres of timber, and eighty acres of apple and peach orchards. Every year this land produces fifty cords of wood, hundreds of bushels of oats and Indian corn, one hundred and fifty bushels of wheat, and several dozen bushels of Irish and sweet potatoes.

B.Y.'s farm teems with livestock, including milch cows, horses, oxen, and dozens of sheep, pigs, cattle, and chickens. These animals contribute to the amount of wool processed on the farm and the two hundred pounds of butter churned there. In addition, a nephew who tenant-farms for B.Y. produces almost eighty gallons of molasses annually (12). Generating all this food requires workers willing to plant and harvest crops, feed animals, muck out the barn, and shear sheep, among countless other jobs. B.Y. employs both laborers who live on his farm and tenant farmers, not all of them relatives, who work other sections of his holdings. Every fall and spring the slaughtering of hogs creates intensive labor for everyone, some of it involving a huge iron kettle, but the results are ham, bacon, lard, and sausage.

After persevering through years of deprivation, B.Y. now easily provides for his family. At age fifty-three he cedes the hardest physical labor to others and serves as manager to his own holdings.

Unfortunately, even amid this comfort, life is still fragile, especially for childbearing women. In addition to their two sons, B.Y. and Martha have a toddler, Cora, and an infant son, Ap (13). But the twenty-nine-year-old Martha falls ill with a fever almost immediately after Ap's birth. As she weakens, so does the baby. Catherine and Rebecca suffer with Martha, reliving the horrible months of their own mother's passing. Seven-year-old John, five-year-old Porter, and three-year-old Cora watch helplessly as their mother becomes increasingly ill. So does B.Y.

Instead of succumbing to consumption, Martha falls prey to an infection that commonly kills women in nineteenth-century America, puerperal fever. While most doctors of Martha's era agree that bacteria cause this fever, they vigorously debate as to how women contract it. In Martha's era, medical science finds such questions unanswerable. The doctors certainly don't realize that they cause this infection in the women they serve. Furthermore, the problem has nothing to do with the rural area in which Martha and B.Y. live;

death rates from puerperal fever are even higher in urban areas (14).

In any case, Martha dies on July 10th, less than two months after giving birth (15). Poor Ap dies a week after his mother (16).

After Martha's death, B.Y. struggles, wondering why giving birth so often kills. Is it punishment, as his son Will might claim? But men die too. His brother Thomas recently departed this life, having never recovered his health from the war (17). B.Y. ponders why he survived the conflict with only a slight injury, while gunshot and disease mangled those around him (18). After much internal debate, he accepts such questions of life and death as unanswerable, even within the terms of his religion, and decides that childbirth simply tests women too severely.

In actuality, many women show great strength during B.Y.'s lifetime. His mother, Polly, bore ten healthy children and was pregnant when she moved by covered wagon from Virginia to Tennessee. In fact, at age eighty-six, Polly Harris still lives (19). Whatever traits guide some humans through traumas that others sometimes cannot withstand, Polly and B.Y. possess them.

The Trophy Wife

AMERICA BARRELS THROUGH most of the 1880s. In the West, settlers voraciously claim Indian land, and a gunfight occurs in Arizona's OK Corral. Further east, the Statue of Liberty arrives from France, Thomas Edison generates electricity, and Mark Twain publishes the first great American novel, *The Adventures of Huckleberry Finn.* The South still struggles, but Booker T. Washington opens the Tuskegee Institute, providing education and job skills for scores of former slaves. In East Tennessee, life follows a more familiar pattern: the bachelor B.Y. Harris busily cares for a half-dozen children. When his daughter Louisa marries John Gammon, her absence hardly impacts the household. His twenty-one-year-old niece Catherine and her eighteen-year-old sister, Rebecca, care for Cora, John, and Porter, and capably run B.Y.'s household. But society approves of remarriage, even for fifty-four-year-olds.

The wealthy, devout farmer with kind blue eyes and a full head of hair can obtain a companion.

Especially if he builds her a new house.

Several months after Martha's death, the Meadow Branch Church of the Brethren hosts a district meeting attended by members of the Cedar Grove Church in Rogersville, about ten miles north of Bean Station. One of the visitors is an educated, twenty-nine-year-old, single woman named Sarah, or Sallie, Webb. The gathering lasts most of the day and includes a meal made boisterous by many playing children. Six-year-old Porter, with his noticeable facial scabs, receives much loving attention from the women of the church. After the meeting, B.Y. helps Sallie mount her horse. His attentions translate clearly enough that on the ride home her friends and family tease her that "poor Porter sure needs a mother" (1). Sallie just laughs.

Daughter of a long-established Tennessee family, Sallie Webb resembles Lucretia and Mary in that her heritage within the state far outstrips B.Y.'s mere forty-six years. In the 1770s her grandfather James McCarty settled in what was then North Carolina, would briefly form the state of Franklin, and later be christened Hawkins County, Tennessee (2). In 1790 James' son William captained a company of the Hawkins Co. Militia, placing him in the same forces as John Lebow, Lucretia's grandfather (3). Sallie's grandmother Mary McCarty Gambill was born in 1792 on the family plantation located on a ridge above the Holston River between Rogersville and Bean Station (4). Four years later, Tennessee became a U.S. state.

With this impressive frontier background and her strong religious beliefs, Sallie refuses to rush into marriage. She is considerably less impressionable than Martha was as a bride. Even at close to age thirty, the point when society considers women almost unmarriageable, she stands firm. When Sallie sees B.Y.'s farm, she admires its fertile beauty but not the frontier-era cabin. After all, she grew up in town. She considers the once-impressive home inadequate for housing a married couple with children ranging in age from infant to adult. So B.Y. enlarges his home. He builds a two-story frame house around the cabin, greatly expanding and updating it. A front porch addition with four small columns creates a more impressive entryway, and large windows in the new rooms allow plenty of light.

Sallie approves, and the two marry in 1881, a year after Martha's death. Reverend Molsbee, Sallie's preacher, performs the ceremony at her father's house in Hawkins County (5). She insists on calling her husband "Bartlet," a name no other wife used.

Sallie and B.Y. are separated by more years than the average couple—she is only a year older than his son Will—but they share common values. Both steadfastly believe in the Brethren church, its concept of pacifism, and its ideals of humbleness and simplicity. Both are industrious. Sallie places a loom on the new front porch and weaves coverlets, creating intricate patterns while forming the textile row by row. Eventually her children inherit these blankets which are considered nicer than quilts. Even though B.Y. employs laborers to help with daily chores on the farm and in the house, Sallie excels at gardening and cooking. She brings more talents to the household than Martha could.

At this point the Bean Station area is thriving also, in fact more so than much of Tennessee. A rebuilt railroad traverses the entire Tennessee Valley, replacing tracks destroyed during the Civil War and enabling visitors to reach the area resorts by rail. One vacation destination in Mooresburg caters to upper East Tennesseans while the Mineral Hill Springs hotel in Bean Station attracts customers from throughout the southeast, partly because it advertises tirelessly in regional newspapers. But the most spectacular establishment sits just outside of town in Tate Springs where Captain Tomlinson successfully created his vision of an elite Victorian resort. Together the local mineral water and mountain air attract a varied clientele who, because of the new railroad, hail from all over the country. These aren't just vacationers; patients with serious health issues such as consumption stay year round.

In order to capitalize on this success, the town of Bean Station curtails its somewhat disreputable reputation by forcibly closing its saloons and barrooms

(6). In their place, Virginia College opens to great fanfare. The school educates both men and women and purchases the old Bean Station Tavern as a dormitory for boarding students. Unfortunately, a fire, possibly arson, destroys the main section of the tavern. One of the side wings escapes unscathed, though, and by itself presents an imposing two-story brick building that preserves at least some of the town's frontier past. With these improvements, one visitor to Bean Station who last saw it during the war remarks upon its progress and comments on the large homes, well-stocked barns, lush fields, and thriving livestock (7).

This prosperity spreads throughout most of Grainger County, ending its postwar malaise and again rousing B.Y.'s entrepreneurial spirit. The postwar blacksmith shop has closed, but he builds a sawmill near his house and begins logging again. His capital and vision build a complete business, from owning the forest to overseeing the lumbering, processing, and selling of the timber. In addition, the more progressive local farmers modernize their practices. When the corn crop fails, a farmers' club is organized and W.S. Shields voted president. The association inspects various specimens of improved seed corn. B.Y. enjoys these meetings and contributes to the club's lively conversation on farming issues. This group hosts a harvest fair that includes horse racing, a show of thoroughbred cattle, ladies horseback riding, a free portrait of the prettiest baby under age two painted by the celebrated Tennessee artist Lloyd Branson, and of course, the sale of horses, cattle, and sheep (8).

After fourteen months of marriage, Sallie gives birth to her and B.Y.'s first child in October of 1882 (9). They name him Samuel after her father, and two and a half years later name their second child Grace. The lives of these children differ greatly from those of B.Y.'s older offspring. The destruction of war doesn't interrupt their childhoods such as Will, Tommy, and Louisa experienced. Unlike John, Porter, and Cora, they escape the poverty and turmoil of the postwar years. Instead they attend Sunday school and in 1888 safely welcome a brother, Yancy Bartlet. Raised by literate parents who both continually impact their lives, they never face hunger or crippling uncertainty. Their father might limp and be well past youth, but he provides guidance and love. They live on a substantial, well-kept farm; a persimmon tree grows on the lane near the house.

During the next several years B.Y.'s sprawling family continues to evolve. Martha's daughter Cora marries and moves to Missouri, but her son John dies at age twenty-one of typhoid fever (10). Three years later B.Y.'s first daughter, Louisa Gammon, perishes in childbirth (11). The first of his children to die as adults, their passing weighs heavily on his heart. B.Y. wonders if John felt slighted during the years-long struggle for postwar prosperity. And Louisa…after he returned from war she didn't recognize him and would hide underneath the kitchen table. For months she lacked a

B.Y.'s children and nieces. From left: Grace, William (Will), Porter, J.T. (Tommy), Prob. Catherine and Rebecca, B.Y., Sallie, Yancy, 1911.

child's natural exuberance. Guiltily B.Y. notes that he was often missing from her life and that his absence was sometimes one of mind, not distance. Now well into middle age, he realizes he has squandered some of life's gifts.

With the freedom and leisure to appreciate his youngest children, perhaps inevitably B.Y. becomes closest to them. With no threat of starvation or poverty, Sam and his half-brother Porter immerse themselves in high-spirited antics. One cold winter evening B.Y. sends Porter to the sawmill to drain the boiler so it won't freeze overnight. But Sam arrives first and hides within the mill's enormous machinery. When Porter reaches to turn the valve that allows the water to drain, Sam grabs his hand, scratches it, and emits a high-pitched scream. Porter sprints to the house, shouting that a cougar attacked him. Sam heartily enjoys the joke while his father chuckles quietly. These two remind him of himself and William, who also relentlessly teased each other.

With Cora living in Missouri, only one of B.Y.'s daughters lives nearby, twelve-year-old Grace, a devout girl who inherits her parents' fair complexions. He dotes on her and calls her "Gracie." While she certainly has chores, her life is one of relative ease compared to most in her neighborhood. She and Louisa's daughter Prissy play dress-up together, then hold mock beauty contests. After B.Y. laughingly refuses to choose a winner, the unfortunate Sallie must decide which girl is prettiest. Any parent can imagine Sallie's diplomacy in choosing the winner as she rewards the girl who that day best practiced kindness and patience. While she is a devout member of the Church of the Brethren who values simplicity, Sallie accepts the girls' imaginative play. She practices a gentler religion than her stepson Will.

As the century turns, the war and its tragedies long behind him, seventy-three-year-old B.Y. mellows into old age. He enjoys attending church and living well with his wife and youngest children. Even with Sam's hijinks and Porter's inevitable retaliations, the household is settled. Following the beliefs of the Brethren Church does limit some of the family's activities. While other well-off locals attend masked balls or catered picnics at the local resorts, the Harris children shun these elaborate parties. But B.Y.'s family does participate in simpler neighborhood events, and he believes in helping others. Twenty-year-old Joseph Barr, a relative to third wife Martha, provides his farm labor. B.Y. also hires newlyweds, with the husband working in the fields and the wife helping Sallie in the house. As much as possible, he shows generosity, not just with those currently in his life but with the community and family from his earlier marriages.

In fact all of Tennessee is finally prospering economically. The turn of the century marks an economic milestone: after thirty-five years the state's crop and land values reach their pre-Civil War levels (12).

CHAPTER 13

The Wheat Thrasher

AT AGE SIXTEEN, Grace Harris finds love in the form of a nineteen-year-old temporary farm worker, one of a group of seasonal laborers who live in neighboring counties but travel throughout the region. In this case B.Y. hires a gang of thrashers to harvest his wheat crop. One worker, Brutus Winkels, connects to B.Y.'s family through Brutus' grandfather, Almarine Wynkel, who moved out of Grainger County after the war (1). Brutus hardly remembers his grandmother Mary, Almarine's first wife and B.Y.'s older sister, who died long ago. But he grew up listening to his grandfather's many stories, some centering on the Harris family. Brutus introduces himself as a distant relative, a grandson of B.Y.'s old friend. He immediately notices blonde, blue-eyed Grace even though she is reserved in the way of well-brought-up young ladies. But there is definite attraction between them, and Brutus makes opportunities to talk with her. For her part, Grace considers the tall, dark-skinned man to be exotically handsome.

But significant differences exist between them. Grace is more educated, and Brutus is unchurched. Most importantly, B.Y. rejects any suggestion that his young Gracie is ready for a serious attachment. He lets this be known, and the much-loved daughter bows to his will. Brutus considers his options. He hates to linger, waiting on Grace to grow up and possibly watching her become attached to another man. Plus he chafes at the implication that he must become a pacifist in order to marry her. No young man likes being told what to do, so in 1901 at age nineteen, Brutus Winkels enlists in the coastal artillery (2). He writes to Grace during his three years in service but also corresponds regularly with another girl. In other words, no promises are made.

Even with Brutus away, Grace keeps busy and enjoys her late teenage years, watching baseball games with her childhood friends, visiting her mother's family in Rogersville, and attending church. Plus, an important family event occurs when her brother Porter marries Ida Isenberg. He courted her with a charming note for her new scrapbook:

"A place for my name in your new album.
A place for my love in your heart.
A place for all in heaven where friends never part."

From left: Porter Harris, Grace Harris, unknown, Eugenia Harris, 1905.

They marry the following year on Christmas day. This event doesn't particularly make Grace feel better, though.

Still, Grainger County experiences exciting times, and not just because of the new century. The local resorts are thriving, with the Tate Springs Hotel catering to an especially elite clientele. No longer just a spa for those with poor health, it draws tourists from across the nation with advertisements claiming "all the refinements of the city hotel, all the ruggedness of the unexplored mountains" (3). In order to vacation there, American's wealthiest citizens flock to Grainger County. The Vanderbilts, Rockefellers, Fords, Firestones, Mellons, and Studebakers arrive at Bean Station in their private rail cars, then ride in plush carriages to nearby Tate Springs (4). The resort spans six thousand acres and contains an eighteen-hole golf course, multiple tennis courts, stables, and a swimming pool. The main building alone contains a ballroom, a bowling alley, and a billiards room. Other amusements available to Tate Springs guests include dancing, playing croquet, and fox hunting. For less mobile fun, the celebrated kitchen staff eagerly packs lunches so guests can enjoy leisurely picnics among the foothills.

The Harris family might not take part in Tate Springs events, but they relish the economic prospects provided by such a neighbor. The hotel is only about thirty minutes away from their house by wagon, and an enterprise of its size requires a vast amount of produce to feed its privileged clients. Only the best will do, and not all commodities can be brought in by train. But Sallie, not B.Y., profits most from the Tate Springs Hotel's business. She furnishes all of the resort's butter, straining it twice to produce a purer product than most local women offer (5). She spends, and saves, the payment as she wishes.

After three years, Brutus Winkels' enlistment in the military ends, and B.Y. and Sallie invite him to dinner. Grace nervously opens the front door when she hears his footsteps. Brutus leans against one of the porch posts, even lankier than before his enlistment. While they exchange greetings, Grace mostly gazes at the wooden planks of the porch flooring, conscious that she wasn't the only girl he wrote while away. But after Brutus catches her attention and grins slowly, she relaxes, suddenly glad her parents invited him. At dinner family jokester Sam enjoys his fried chicken, then sneaks his leftover bones onto Brutus' plate. He then loudly comments that Brutus must be starving to have eaten so much. Everyone laughs, and sitting at the head of the table, B.Y. silently concedes that his youngest daughter will soon marry.

But an issue remains for Grace: religion. After Brutus' return, she attends an annual meeting of the Brethren in Bristol, Virginia, with her brother Porter and two friends from church. In addition to the church functions, the three young women enjoy a vacation in town while shopping, getting their picture made, and having ice cream. This trip to a religious gathering also clarifies Grace's priorities to any attentive friend. Brutus Winkels soon takes the hint, joins the Church of the Brethren, and marries Grace in November of 1905 at her father's house (6). B.Y. genuinely likes Brutus and helps the couple start out, selling them part of his land with generous terms for repayment.

With Porter and Grace now both married, their twenty-four-year-old brother Sam chafes at his settled routine. Enthralled by Brutus' tales of life in the service, he craves adventure. But having been raised in the Brethren church, Sam genuinely believes in a peace-seeking life, so he rejects the armed forces as an option. However, stories of the Rocky Mountains fascinate him, so he decides to move west. B.Y. helps by giving him a hundred dollars of his inheritance, and a second family connection also facilitates Sam's plans. B.Y. has always kept in touch with his varying and far-flung children. Lucretia's oldest child, Will, and Sam's half-sister Cora, Martha's only girl, now live with their families in Colorado (7). Sam contacts Will and arranges to stay with him for a few weeks while he settles into his new life. Because he is on a budget, Sam travels across country with a wagon train instead of by rail. He walks as much as possible during the long trip but must also ride on the rickety and terribly uncomfortable wagon. When he finally arrives in Colorado, Sam swears he will never make that trip again.

Samuel Harris ca. 1905

In fact he soon puts down roots, marrying Elsie Ure, the telephone operator who helped him contact Will while planning the trip west. She found Sam's deep voice and southern accent intriguing over the phone, and his lively personality captivates her once they meet. They soon produce two fine sons, but their first years together are trying. They live with Elsie's parents, then in a tarpaper shack, then a tent.

Still, Sam writes home with glorious descriptions of Colorado and the Rocky Mountains. In 1910 he convinces his brother Yancy to visit. At that point he and Elsie live near Will, which allows B.Y.'s oldest and youngest sons to get acquainted (8). Will's stories of growing up with a younger B.Y. astound Sam and Yancy. Through him they envision their father as a young man living though war, one who endured staggering troubles. In turn, Will realizes he hasn't seen his father in years and soon returns to Tennessee for a last visit.

CHAPTER 14

Last of the Embers

B.Y. AND SALLIE enter a new phase in their lives in 1911 when Yancy returns to Tennessee and marries Dixie Wright. For the first time in fifty-seven years, no children live in B.Y.'s home. Of course, at eighty-four years old he deserves the quiet. The decades-old limp has worsened and he has a troubling cough, especially at night. But he still enjoys a lively old age and spends much time puttering around the large barn which was always his refuge away from the busy household. He and Sallie participate in community events and donate land for a new Meadow Branch Church building (1). Even a congregation that values simplicity agrees that the reconstruction-era log cabin needs replacing. B.Y. adds to his farm's acreage, purchasing a nearby tract of land known to have once belonged to John Lebow (2). He wants to keep as much of the historic farm intact as possible.

B.Y. also corresponds regularly with friends and family, including John Murray, long-term pastor of the Meadow Branch Church. The men exchange opinions on life and politics, and hope that America will remain impartial toward the ongoing conflict between Germany and other European countries. Murray calls war "a curse to the human race in the downward tendency it has in morality and religion, and the great suffering of the noncombatants" (3). Maybe others have forgotten the horrors of the Civil War, but these men still remember. Years after the war the reasons why B.Y. joined the Church of the Brethren still resonate for him.

At age fifty-eight Sallie's energy outpaces that of her husband. With the money earned from selling butter, she purchases new household furniture from Ireland and updated appliances such as an iron fueled by kerosene. In contrast, like most women of the area, in order to iron her family's clothes, Grace must heat several solid irons on a stove. She uses one until it cools, then returns it to the heat source and picks up another. But the iron's temperature fluctuates throughout the process, making it easier to ruin the cloth than with her mother's updated appliances.

In fact, once she marries, Grace leaves a home of wealth and relative ease for the unending chores of a small farm. As a young couple, she and Brutus expect some hardship, and he earns extra money by being the local census taker in 1910. But much of

Grace's stress occurs because of relentless pregnancies. After marrying in November, she gives birth to their first child, Elsie, ten months later in September. Other children follow in almost exact two-year intervals: Gladys, then Ora, then Lucille (4). Childbirth kills less frequently than it did in B.Y.'s youth, but even this medical improvement reveals a problem. Grace survives her children's births, but with birth control unheard of, she is almost always either pregnant or nursing a child. The quick succession of offspring exhausts her physically and emotionally.

In addition to childcare, Grace tends the family's chickens, cleans house, and keeps the kitchen garden. She prepares the chicken for frying, picks the vegetables, cooks dinner, and later cans the garden's overflow. In contrast to her mother, she and Brutus don't employ servants. Many women of her era endure similar lives, meeting these challenges with quiet perseverance and selflessness. Religion provides one comfort to Grace since her family attends the same Brethren church as her parents. She keeps other priorities, setting aside money made from selling eggs so the children can be educated.

Now in his late eighties, B.Y. begins thinking seriously about his estate. Of all his land, none is more significant than the homestead, with its house, barns, mill, and other buildings. The farm's natural spring exists in a community famous for them. In fact the farmstead and its surrounding acreage are as coveted as they were the day his father David bought them sixty years before. None of B.Y.'s children remember a time when the homestead was not Harris land, and all value it emotionally. The local farmers among them know what this jewel could do for their lives. In truth B.Y. considers that his inheritance to these older children was dispatched long ago when he distributed the money from their guardianships. Plus, he has always been generous, and most of his children owe him money. The amounts range from less than fifty dollars by Porter and Cora to almost a thousand by Will, fifteen hundred by Tommy, and over two thousand by Grace (5). This money equals $27,000 worth of purchasing power in modern dollars and actually reflects the value of land bought from her father when she married (6).

B.Y. makes his will, dividing his land in two for Grace and Yancy, with Grace receiving the section that contains the farm. He insists that he and Sallie have the right to live there until they die (7).

With this job taken care of, B.Y. enjoys his old age. In 1912 a Model T chugs noisily down the lane in front of his house and astounds him with the realities of modernity. Because of its many wealthy clients, the Ford Company established one of America's earliest automobile dealerships at the Tate Springs Resort. Many changes have occurred in America since B.Y. was a settler's son, and they have accelerated since the Civil War's end. As he watches the car, B.Y. wryly contemplates that he has outlasted his own era, similar to how he outlived so many comrades and loved ones. Still, he enjoys his role as a community patriarch and often functions as an informal bank. When someone asks to borrow money, he jots down the man's name and the amount borrowed on scrap paper, then scrupulously destroys the note once he is repaid. Perhaps it is this practice that makes him so universally admired.

With Grace and her family living nearby, he enjoys seeing them often. All the grandchildren consider him an important figure in their lives, but Elsie, Grace's oldest, takes to her grandfather the most closely. She enjoys listening to him tell stories about the past. He confides to her about the only lie he ever told that he did not repent of, the time he promised the Confederate recruiters that he would go home for his rifle and return to their camp. Somewhat mischievously he sets granddaughters Elsie, Gladys, and Ora to picking cotton. The other girls don't mind the job, but eight-year-old Gladys detests the hot, dirty work and vows to leave the farm as an adult and live in the city.

In 1917 after a respite of over four years, Grace bears another child, her first son, Lon. In two years she will give birth to another daughter, Bertha Sue, then daughter Reece, and later a son, Roge. The stress proves too much for her, and after eleven years of marriage, she moves her family into her father's house. Even with it established that Grace will inherit the homestead, this move proves controversial. B.Y. is elderly, eighty-nine years old, and wants to be taken care of. Sixty-three-year-old Sallie, however, resists conceding her household to someone else, even a daughter. Grace sees herself as helping her elderly parents and settling into the house she will inherit. Sallie feels pushed out of her own home. Stresses simmer as Sallie's home suddenly includes five adored but active grandchildren, and two farm wives divide the daily chores. In order to avoid confrontation, Sallie visits Sam and his family in Colorado, boarding a train for the journey amid tense good-byes. In her mother's absence Grace adjusts to being the home's main housekeeper and cook. But conflicts remain unresolved between mother and daughter, between husband and wife.

When America joins the world war in Europe, the Harris family holds steadfastly to their pacifist beliefs. B.Y. refuses to see war as the way to solve problems, and he frequently comments on the senselessness of the Civil War, mentioning his two brothers who died and the challenges his family and the community endured. Grace and her siblings often heard of these trials during their childhood. Thus when Yancy is drafted by the U.S. Army, B.Y. encourages his youngest son to apply for an appeal. Luckily the army bypasses Yancy because of his three young children, and he is spared further conflict between his religion and his love of country.

Unfortunately, as in the Civil War, during World War I more soldiers die from disease than from battle. But this time civilians must also deal with illness, in fact, with a pandemic.

In America the outbreak of influenza begins in Kansas. It sweeps rapidly through urban and rural areas, affecting all age groups but most cruelly targeting healthy young adults. Influenza spreads and kills so quickly that within a year the average life expectancy of Americans drops by twelve years. The largest number of national fatalities comes late in 1918 with almost two hundred thousand deaths in October alone. Amid justifiable fear, drastic steps are taken; merchants cancel Christmas sales to discourage crowds. But the deaths continue across the United States into the new year.

In Grainger County, Yancy Bartlet Harris, B.Y.'s healthy twenty-three-year-old namesake, succumbs to the flu in January of 1919. Far away in Colorado, Sallie is inconsolable when she hears the news. She writes B.Y. and tells him that she wants to return home and help the newly widowed Dixie care for her young children (8). But everyone knows that being in crowds increases the risk of contracting the disease. B.Y. replies, telling her to wait with Sam's family until the epidemic ends, that he fears she will catch the disease on the train. This caution backfires, though. Sallie dies of influenza on February 22, 1919 at Sam's home in Colorado (9). Hiding from an epidemic such as this one just isn't possible.

The Winkels family. From left: Elsie, Grace Harris Winkels, Ora, Brutus Seabern Winkels, Gladys, 1911.

B.Y.'s grieves intensely for his wife of almost thirty-eight years. He had privately thought she was the wife who would outlive him. When Sam asks about arrangements for his mother, B.Y. tells his son not to bury her in Colorado. She must come home to her beloved Tennessee. Sending her body east on the train requires elaborate arrangements. Friends help with the complex process by overseeing a transfer at Morristown and then transporting the body from the Bean Station depot to the church. Of course the funeral takes place at Meadow Branch Church, its sanctuary full of mourners in a last tribute to Sallie. As for B.Y., the old soldier comments that she is the prettiest dead person he ever saw.

After Sallie's death, at age ninety-two, having outlived four wives, five children, and all his siblings but Jim, B.Y. begins to decline (10).

When he hears the news of his father's illness, Sam buys a secondhand car, a Nash. He immediately starts out across America with Elsie and their children, determined to see B.Y. one last time. The trip proves eventful. Their vehicle struggles on the poorly maintained roads, and in rural Missouri it gets stuck in the mud. Sam manages to find volunteers to help free the car, but it sustains considerable damage. Even worse, he lacks funds to pay for repairs. Warily he approaches the local bank. The manager resists loaning money to an out-of-state traveler, but Sam persists. The manager finally has Sam line his children up against a wall in the bank. He takes their picture, then gives Sam a loan, commenting that if Sam neglects to repay the money, he can be tracked down through his children's faces.

At least this is how Sam tells the story once he reaches Tennessee.

Unfortunately, even Sam's humor can't alter reality, and B.Y. declines throughout the summer and into the fall. Even the months of waiting are eventful for the household. Sam's sons Jimmy and Amos begin their school year in Tennessee, and when his wife Elsie catches diphtheria, authorities quarantine the entire household. Grace does her best to take care of her dying father, her husband and children, and her brother's family. One day as she untangles six-year-old Lucile's hair, she spots head lice. This infestation violates Grace's standards of hygiene, and she often cautions her children not to wear someone else's hat for just this reason. Lucile earnestly promises her mother that she did not wear a schoolmate's hat but concedes that she might have held one over her head for a moment. The improbable story makes Grace laugh, even amid her stress and despair.

But such lighthearted moments are rare. After supper when the day's chores are finished, Grace and Sam's families tend to congregate on the porch under the shade trees. Neighbors often hail them from the road, inquiring after B.Y.'s health and passing along news of community members' deaths and of their recoveries. One such evening Grace's grief over her mother's death and the conflict between them at the time overwhelms her. With her younger brother Yancy dead and her father ailing, she faces irrevocable change. Brutus tries to console her, reaching over from his chair to hold her hand, but the grim situation engulfs him too. After a few moments Grace abruptly stands, claiming that sitting down made her cry. Thus Grace soldiers on, completing her many chores and trying to find solace in her husband, children, and brother. Like her father before her, Grace must come to terms with the reality that she will be one who lives.

B.Y. often rests in the barn away from the heat and noise of the house, barely acknowledging the presence of others. After a months-long decline, on October 12, 1919 Bartlet Yancy Harris dies in his sleep (11). During a long life he overcame many challenges, transforming from settler to entrepreneur, farmer to soldier, newlywed to widow. He endured carnage and loss, yet persevered, retaining his ambition, his compassion, his soul. Most importantly, when B.Y. dies, a loving family mourns for him…and buries him…near Bean Station, East Tennessee.

Acknowledgments

This book was written to document the facts of B.Y.'s life. The endnotes are designed to fulfill the work that Elsie Winkels Samsel began and spare future generations from re-researching. The author wrote in the creative non-fiction genre, making assumptions of motive and character. She apologizes if any family member takes exception to one. Family stories form much of this narrative, with the more important ones also documented. Many thanks to my mother, Nancy Shaver Currence, who was born on the family homestead and provided an invaluable sounding board. Thanks also to my father, Earl Layman, who instilled in me the pride in being a Tennessean that permeates this work. Delma Winkels, Ruth Valentine, Col. Dean Rich, Ret., Keith Rich, Addison West, Dr. Douglas Layman, and Deloris Wilder all donated invaluable information, time and energy to this project. Thanks also to "the group" for continually pushing me. Yes, I appreciate it. In addition, Stevvie Cook of the Grainger County

Archives was wonderfully helpful and patient during years of research. Thanks especially to my husband, Gary, who has an uncanny ability to know just when to back out of a working writer's office. Without his support this book would never have been written. Much love goes to my sons, Logan and Landon, who make their mother extremely proud.

Endnotes

Chapter One: Bean's Station

1) Samsel, Elsie Winkles. Cassette Tape. July 4, 1987.

2) *War of 1812 Pension Application Files Index.* "David Harris." Pension # WC 26779. Original Source: National Archives and Records Administration. Ancestry.com. Web. May 22, 2013. David served under Cap. J. Adams.

3) "David Harris." *Virginia, Marriages, 1740-1850. Ancestry.com.* Rpt. from: Dodd, Jordan R., et al. *Early American Marriages: Virginia to 1850.* Bountiful, UT, USA: Precision Indexing Pub. ancestry.com Operations Inc, 1999. Web. May 22, 2013. Exact date of marriage: December 21, 1816. Both were both born in 1794.

4) McGinnis, Robert A. *In Sweet Remembrance: the Cemeteries of Grainger County, Tennessee*

Vol. III. 2008. p. 162. Exact date of birth: November 25, 1826. On various documents "Bartlet" is also spelled as "Bartlett."

5) "Harris, David." Tennessee, *Early Tax List Records, 1783-1895.* 1836. *Ancestry.com.* Original data: Early Tax Lists of Tennessee. Microfilm, 12. The Tennessee State Library and Archives, Nashville, Tennessee. Ancestry. com Operations. 2013. Web. May 22, 2013.

6) United States. Census Bureau. *1850 Census, District 2, Grainger County, Tennessee.* "David Harris" *Ancestry.com.* Ancestry.com 2010. Web. February 3, 2013.

7) Vial, Rebecca. "Wilderness Road" *The Tennessee Encyclopedia of History and Culture*, Version 2.0. The University of Tennessee Press, 2002-2013. Web. January 5, 2014.

8) Coffee, Ken. "History of Bean Station." *Town of Bean Station.* Town of Bean Station, Tennessee. 2013-14. Web. May 22, 2014.

9) *U.S. Compiled Service Records, Post-Revolutionary War Volunteer Soldiers 1784-1811.* Ancestry.com. 2011. Web. May 6, 2013. The spellings used are "John Leebo" in 1793, "John Lebow" in 1797, and "Lebeau" when paid in 1794. (Marriage: *U.S. and International Marriages* 1560-1900. Source number: 2480.032. Web.)

10) State of Tennessee. Land Grant, "John Lebo." October 5, 1827. MS. Family provided copy of original signed by then-governor Sam Houston. Spelling used is "Lebo" and "Libo." At the time the spelling of names was often unstandardized. When Lebow pays Grainger Co. taxes his name is spelled "Leabo" in 1799, "Lebow" in 1805, and "Lebo" in 1810.

11) Samsel, Elsie Winkles. Cassette Tape. July 4, 1987.

12) United States. Census Bureau. *1830 Census, Grainger, Tennessee.* "John Lebo" Ancestry. com. NARA Series: M19; Roll Number: 180; Family History Film: 0024538. Page: 402; Ancestry.com, 2010. Web. July 20, 2014.

13) Gray, William. Accounting of the Estate of John Adam Lebow. ND. MS hard copy. Also Measuring Worth Calculator for 2013. Measuringworth.com. June 9, 2014. Lebow information comes from family-provided hard copies. Date of death: McGinnis, Robert A. *In Sweet Remembrance: the Cemeteries of Grainger County, Tennessee* Vol. III. 2008. p.157.

14) Gray, William. "Account of the Sale of the Estate of John Lebow." October 20, 1840. MS hard copy.

15) United States. *Full Pension File-Civil War.* "Harris, Bartlet, Yancy." General Affidavit. 27

Nov. 1891. National Archives and Records Administration. September 20, 2013. Print.

16) "Booker M. Harris." *Illinois Marriages 1851-1900, Jan. 10 1853*. Ancestry.com Jordan Dodd and Liahona Research, comp. Ancestry.com Operations Inc, 2005. Web. June 2013.

17) "Booken M. Harris." *U.S. Civil War Draft Registrations Records 1863-1865 for Marion, Illinois*. Ancestry.com. Rpt. from National Archives and Records Administration. Consolidated Lists of Civil War Draft Registration Records. Record Group 110. Ancestry.com Operations, 2010. Web. June 12, 2014. He has a later marriage to "Mary" and dies in Newton Co., Missouri in 1908. See the 1880 Newton, Missouri census.

18) Douthat, James. *Grainger Co. Tn Various Records 1796-1848*. 1996. East TN Historical Center. p. 50.

19) "Almarine M. Winkle." *U.S., American Volunteer Soldiers, Mexican War, 1845-1848*. Ancestry.com. Ancestry.com operations 2013. Web. July 10, 2013.

20) *North Carolina and Tennessee, Early Land Records 1753-1931*. Ancestry.com. Rpt. from Tennessee Land Office Records, 1783-1927, Record Group 50. 1849. Ancestry.com. 2013. Web. June 6, 2013. Also, Samsel's notes say B.Y. lived in the homestead since before 1850.

Chapter Two: Name Change

1) North Carolina and TN, Early Land Records 1753-1931. "David Harris." Ancestry.com. Rpt. From Tennessee Land Office Records, 1783-1927. East TN Land Grants. Roll 88, Book 31, p. 287. Ancestry.com 2013. Web. June 18, 2013.

2) United States. Census Bureau. *1850 Census, District 2, Grainger County, Tennessee.* "David Harris" Ancestry.com. Ancestry.com 2010. Web. February 3, 2013. Both David and his hired man identify themselves as "tobacconists."

3) B.Y., Thomas, James and William are all noted as blue-eyed, with fair hair and skin, in their Civil War discharge papers.

4) United States. Census Bureau. *U.S. Federal Census-Slave Schedules, 1850.* "William Gray." Ancestry.com. May 6, 2014. Gray has eight slaves at this point.

5) *Selected U.S. Federal Census Non-Population Schedules, 1850-1880* "William Gray." Ancestry. com. Ancestry.com 2010. Web. May 6, 2014.

6) United States. Census Bureau. *1850 Census, District 12, Hawkins County, Tennessee.* "William Gray." Ancestry.com. Ancestry.com 2010. Web. 3 February, 2013. On this census Lucretia and Mary are incorrectly identified as being, respectively, nineteen and

twenty-three. Sarah is sixteen and Margaret thirteen. Ten years later, B.Y. Harris Grainger Co. census identifies Lucretia's age as thirty-two. Also, Lucretia's tombstone states that she was born March 5, 1827. See McGinnis, 162.

7) *U.S. National Homes for Disabled Volunteer Soldiers, 1866-1938* "Stokley S. Gray." Ancestry.com. Ancestry.com 2007. Web. July 1, 2014. The author assumes that Lucretia shares this dark coloring with her brother. The description, which includes "dark skin," is the only support the author could find for a relative's assertion that the Gray daughters were Melungeon.

8) United States. Census Bureau. *1860 Census, District 9, Grainger County, Tennessee.* "B.Y. Harris." Ancestry.com. Roll: *M653_1250*; Page: *475*; Image: *567*; Family History Library Film: *805250*. ancestry.com 2009. Web. February 3, 2013. Elsie Samsel's notes specify the wedding date: September 23, 1852.

9) United States. Census Bureau. *1860 Census, District 12, Hawkins County, Tennessee.* "William Harris." Ancestry.com. Roll: *M653_1255*; Page: *135*; Image: *275*; Family History Library Film: *805255*. Ancestry.com 2009. Web. August 5, 2013. Elsie Samsel's notes also identify Mary Gray as the widow of B.Y.'s brother William.

10) Nancy Shaver Currence recounted this family story. Since the name of the bridegroom who refused the slave has been lost, it was probably not B.Y. William is the next logical candidate.

11) United States. Census Bureau. *1860 Census,* "B.Y. Harris."

12) United States. Census Bureau. *1870 Census, District 9, Grainger County, Tennessee.* "B.Y. Harris" Ancestry.com. Roll: *M593_1530*; Page: *104A*; Image: *212*; Family History Library Film: *553029*. Ancestry.com 2009. Web. June 17, 2013.

13) United States. Census Bureau. *1860 Census,* "B.Y. Harris."

14) Harris, B.Y. *Tobacco Business Ledger.* February 10, 1856 through May 5, 1861. MS. Hard Copy.

15) United States. Census Bureau. *1860 Census,* "B.Y. Harris." Samsel's written notes on B.Y. Harris describe him as a "tobacconist, farmer, trader in land and timber."

16) "Seven Ways to Compute the Relative Value of a U.S. Dollar Amount." *Measuring Worth.* measuringworth.com. June 2013.

17) Lansford, Jack. Letter to William G. Harris. January 30, 1857. TS of old MS.

18) United States. United States Department of the Interior Bureau of Pensions. *Full Pension File-Civil War.* "Harris, James P." paperwork #3-389. 4 May, 1915. National Archives and

Records Admin. 1 Sept. 2013. Print. The date of marriage is November 4, 1858.

19) United States Census Bureau. *1860 Census, District 9, Grainger County, Tennessee.* "David Harris" Ancestry.com. Roll: *M653_1250*; Page: *478*; Image: *572*; Family History Library Film: *805250*. Ancestry.com 2009. Web. February 3, 2013.

Chapter Three: The War Begins at Home

1) Lansford, Jack. Letter to David Harris. 19 March, 1861. MS. The author searched in slave schedules and Census records for proof of slave ownership. Samsel's tape also specifies that no Harrises owned slaves.

2) United States. Census Bureau. *1860 Census, District 12, Hawkins County, Tennessee.* "William Gray." Ancestry.com. Roll: *M653_1255*; Page: *135*; Image: *276*; Family History Library Film: *805255*. ancestry.com 2009. Web. August 7, 2013.

3) "Seven Ways to Compute the Relative Value of a U.S. Dollar Amount." *Measuring Worth.* measuringworth.com. December 2013.

4) *The Blue and Gray from Hawkins County: 1861-1865.* Compiled by Johnston, Shelia Weems. Angelfire.com. Mar. 8, 2014. Web. June 12, 2014.

5) McKenzie, Robert Tracey. "Oh, Ours Is a Deplorable Condition." *The Civil War in Appalachia: Collected Essays.* Eds. Kenneth W. Noe and Shannon H. Wilson. Knoxville: University of Tennessee Press. 1997. p. 202.

6) "8th Tennessee Volunteer Infantry Regiment-USA." *The Blue and Gray: the Federals.* Compiled by Sheila Weems Johnston. 3 vols. Rogersville: Hawkins Co. Genealogical and Historical Society. 1995. p. 232.

7) McKenzie. p. 204.

8) Valentine, Ruth. Telephone Interview. June 2, 2013. The author heard several versions of this story from different family members. The culprit was identified as "foragers" in one story and "Union troops" in another. At this point in the war, the foragers would have probably been Confederate.

9) Fisher, Noel. *War at Every Door: Partisan Politics & Guerrilla Violence in East Tennessee,* 1860-1869. Chapel Hill: The University of North Carolina Press. 1997, p. 87-88.

10) Fisher. 88.

11) *Memphis Daily Appeal.* 3 July, 1862. Image #1. Chronicling America: Historic American Newspapers. Library of Congress. Chroniclingamerica.gov. Web. May 21, 2014.

12) Miller, Ernest I. "The Valley of East Tennessee in the Civil War." November 1957. *Cincinnati*

Civil War Roundtable rpt. 1996. Web. May 14, 2014.

13) Samsel, Elsie Winkles. Cassette Tape. July 4, 1987. Several family members shared close versions of this story.

14) "8th Tennessee Volunteer Infantry Regiment." *Tennesseans in the Civil War: Federal Infantry Units.* Tngenweb.org. TNGenweb Project. July, 14 2004. Web. June 1, 2013. Also see B.Y. Harris Pension Records.

Chapter Four: The 8th Regiment of Tennessee

1) McKenzie, Robert Tracey. "Oh, Ours Is a Deplorable Condition." *The Civil War in Appalachia: Collected Essays.* Eds. Kenneth W. Noe and Shannon H. Wilson. Knoxville: University of Tennessee Press. 1997. 202. Print.

2) Bare, Joseph A. Letter to Elizabeth Bare. 5 Oct. 1863. Rpt. in *The Blue and Gray: the Federals.* Compiled by Sheila Weems Johnston. 3 vols. Rogersville: Hawkins Co. Genealogical and Historical Society. 1995. 174. Print. Alternative spellings are "Barr" and "Bear," but the pronunciation is always "Bare" as per Elsie W. Samsel cassette tape.

3) "8th Tennessee Volunteer Infantry Regiment-USA." *The Blue and Gray: the Federals.* Compiled by Sheila Weems Johnston. 3 vols.

Rogersville: Hawkins Co. Genealogical and Historical Society. 1995. p. 230. Related sources list William G. Harris as age 24, but this is either a separate person or more probably a clerical error. Some company muster-in rolls do refer to William G. Harris, age 33.

4) *Report of the Adjutant General of the State of Tennessee: of the military forces of the state, from 1861 to 1866*. "Eighth Regiment. Company I" for "James P. Harris." Ancestry. com. Web. Ancestry.com Operations, 2011. January 9, 2013. See also *The Blue and Gray: the Federals* compiled by Johnston.

5) *Report of the Adjutant General of the State of Tennessee: of the military forces of the state, from 1861 to 1866*. "Eighth Regiment. Company I" for "Harris, Thomas L." Ancestry. com. Web. Ancestry.com Operations, 2011. January 9, 2013. Thomas first shows on a muster roll in Nov. 1863.

6) *U.S. Civil War Soldiers 1861-65* about "Stokley C. (S) Gray." Film #M392 roll 6. Ancestry.com. Ancestry.com Operations, 2011. Web. June 18, 2014.

7) *Report of the Adjutant General of the State of Tennessee of the Military Forces of the State, 1861-1866*. "Eighth Regiment. Company I" for "Joseph P. Barr." Ancestry.com. Web. Ancestry. com Operations, 2011. January 9, 2013. This

document spells Joseph and Robert's last name as "Barr," as does the 1850 Hawkins Co. census for Joseph's father, Peter. The National Park Service database, *U.S. Civil War Soldiers,* still referencing the 8th regiment, Co. I, uses "Bare" with "Bear" as an alternate. Joseph was "Bare" when he married Elizabeth (Hicks) on December 24th, 1857 (*TN State Marriages*) but they are referenced as "Bar" on the 1860 Hancock Co. census. His letter home and descendents use "Bare," the spelling I have chosen to use. His sister Martha uses "Barr."

8) *U.S. Civil War Soldiers, 1861-1865,* nps.gov. United States National Park Service. 2013. Web. December 14, 2013. "James B. Haris" and "Permenius Haris" refer to James B. Harris and Permilius Harris. James B. Harris is married to Susan; William Long is married to Elizabeth. Rebecca's husband, Peter Meeks, is mentioned in Bare's letter as being in Company I of the 8th Regiment.

9) Freemon, Frank R. *Gangrene and Glory.* Chicago: University of Illinois Press. 2001, p. 205.

10) "8th Tennessee Regiment Infantry." *A Compendium of the War of the Rebellion. Part 3.* Compiled by Frederick H. Dyer. civilwararchive.com. The Civil War Archive. January 24 2009. Web. June 12, 2013.

11) "8th Tennessee Volunteer Infantry Regiment." *Tennesseans in the Civil War*. VolunteerGEnWeb Tennesseans in the Civil War Project. 2005. Web. January 20, 2014. All 8th Tennessee Regiment troop movements are taken from this source unless otherwise noted.

12) Taylor, Paul. Book review of *The Knoxville Campaign: Burnside and Longstreet in East Tennessee by Earl Hess*. Civilwarnews. com. *The Civil War News*. April 2013. Web. November 4, 2013.

13) United States Army. "8th Reg't Tenn. Infantry Company I Muster roll for William G. Harris." Nov. and Dec. 1863. Provided by: U.S. National Archives and Records. Print.

14) Hess, Earl J. *The Knoxville Campaign: Burnside and Longstreet in East Tennessee*. Knoxville: University of Tennessee Press. 2012. Ebook. 18.

15) United States Census Bureau. *1850 Census, District 12, Hawkins County, Tennessee*. "Peter Barr." Ancestry.com. Ancestry.com 2010. Web. February 3, 2013. 1850 U.S. Census records for Grainger Co., Tennessee. Spelled as "Bar" 1860. William Gray is on the same census sheets.

16) Bare, Joseph A. Letter to Elizabeth Bare. October 5, 1863. Rpt. in *The Blue and Gray: the Federals*. Compiled by Sheila Weems

Johnston. 3 vols. Rogersville: Hawkins Co. Genealogical and Historical Society. 1995. 174. Print.

17) Bare. 174.

18) Davis, Stephen. "Atlanta Campaign" *New Georgia Encyclopedia*. Georgiaencyclopedia.org. Georgia Humanities Council. June 5, 2014. Web. 14 June 2014.

19) Fisher, Noel. *War at Every Door: Partisan Politics & Guerrilla Violence in East Tennessee, 1860-1869.* Chapel Hill: The University of North Carolina Press. 1997, 147. Print.

20) Fisher. 148.

21) Fisher. 148.

Chapter Five: Battling Longstreet

1) *McKenzie, Robert Tracey. "Oh, Ours Is a Deplorable Condition." The Civil War in Appalachia: Collected Essays. Eds. Kenneth W. Noe and Shannon H. Wilson. Knoxville: University of Tennessee Press. 1997. 203. Print.*

2) Fisher, Noel. *War at Every Door: Partisan Politics & Guerrilla Violence in East Tennessee, 1860-1869.* Chapel Hill: The University of North Carolina Press. 1997, 148-9. Print.

3) Moyar, Mark. *A Question of Command: Counterinsurgency from the Civil War to Iraq.* Yale University Press: 2010. p.25.

4) Samsel, Elsie Winkles. Cassette Tape. July 4, 1987.

5) Carter, S.P. Federal Provost-Marshal General of East Tennessee. Letter to Brig. Gen. Edward E. Potter, Chief of Staff, Army of the Ohio. *December 19, 1863*. Rpt. In *OR*, Ser. I, Vol. 31, pt. III. 447-448. PDF.

6) Bible, Thomas, Cap. "Military History and Travels of Captain Thomas Bible." Rpt. in *The Blue and Gray: the Federals*. Compiled by Sheila Weems Johnston. Rogersville: Hawkins Co. Genealogical and Historical Society. 1995. p.165. Print.

7) Hardy, William E. Ed. *Knoxville's Voices of the Civil War: A Documentary Reader*. teachamericahistory.org. Teaching American History. 2010. PDF. July 3, 2014. 2.

8) Seymour, Digby. *Divided Loyalties*. 3rd ed. UT Press: Knoxville, 1963. 262. Print. The 8th TN is part of Hoskins Provisional Brigade.

9) Seymour. 262.

10) Huddard, William A. Dec. 13, 1863, William A. Huddard papers, Special Collections, U.T. Libraries in *Knoxville's Voices of the Civil War: A Documentary Reader*. Hardy, William E. Ed. p. 20. teachamericahistory.org. 2010. PDF. July 3, 2014.

11) Hess, Earl J. *The Knoxville Campaign: Burnside and Longstreet in East Tennessee*. Knoxville:

University of Tennessee Press. 2012. Ebook. p. 214.

12) Hess. 215.

13) "8th Tennessee Volunteer Infantry Regiment." *Tennesseans in the Civil War: Federal Infantry Units.* Tngenweb.org. Rpt from *Tennesseans in the Civil War Vol. I.* 1964 TNGenweb Project. July 14, 2004. Web. June 1, 2013.

14) Hess. 176.

15) Fowler, John D. "We can never live in a southern confederacy." Sister States, Enemy States. Eds. Dollar, Whiteaker, and Dickinson. Univ. Press of KY: Lexington. Kindle. 2009, 107.

16) McKenzie. 205.

17) *Memphis Daily Appeal.* 17 Mar. 1864. Chronicling America: Historic American Newspapers. Library of Congress. chroniclingamerica.loc.gov. ND. Web. May 21, 2014.

18) Bible p. 165 and Bare, Robert p.175 in Johnston.

19) Johnston, Sheila Weems. Commentary In *The Blue and Gray: the Federals.* Rogersville: Hawkins Co. Genealogical and Historical Society. 1995. p.175. Print.

20) Bare, Joseph A. Letter to Elizabeth Bare. 5 Oct. 1863. Rpt. in *The Blue and Gray: the Federals.* Compiled by Sheila Weems Johnston. 3 vols. Rogersville: Hawkins Co. Genealogical and Historical Society. 1995. 175. Print.

21) "Eighth Regiment. Company I." Report of the Adjutant General of the State of Tennessee: of the military forces of the state, from 1861 to 1866. Ancestry.com. Ancestry.com Operations, 2011. Web. September 1, 2013. See also James Harris' pension records, promotion.

22) Bible in Johnston. 165.

23) United States Army. "8th Reg't Tenn. Infantry Company I Muster rolls for Bartlett Y. Harris and Thomas L. Harris." Mar. and April, May and June 1864. Provided by: U.S. National Archives and Records. Print.

24) United States Army. "8th Reg't Tenn. Infantry Company I Muster rolls for Bartlett Y. Harris and Thomas L. Harris." July and Aug., 1864. Provided by: U.S. National Archives and Records. Print.

Chapter Six: The Thick of War: Atlanta

1) "Casualties and Costs of the Civil War." *The Gilder Lehrman Institute of American History*. The Gilder Lehrman Institute of American History. Gilderlehrman.com 2009-2014. Web. July 1, 2014.

2) "8th Regiment Infantry." *A Compendium of the War of the Rebellion. Part 3*. Compiled by Frederick H. Dyer. civilwararchive.com. The Civil War Archive. January 25, 2009. Web. June 12, 2013.

3) McKenzie, Robert Tracey. "Oh, Ours Is a Deplorable Condition." *The Civil War in Appalachia: Collected Essays*. Eds. Kenneth W. Noe and Shannon H. Wilson. Knoxville: University of Tennessee Press. 1997. 206. Print.

4) Fisher, Noel. *War at Every Door: Partisan Politics & Guerrilla Violence in East Tennessee, 1860-1869*. Chapel Hill: The University of North Carolina Press. 1997, 134. Print.

5) Fowler, John D. "We can never live in a southern confederacy." *Sister States, Enemy States*. Eds. Dollar, Whiteaker, and Dickinson. Univ. Press of KY: Lexington. Kindle. 2009, 109.

6) Carter, S.P. Federal Provost-Marshal General of East Tennessee. Letter to Lieut. Col. G. M. Bascom, Assistant Adjutant-Gen., Dept of the Ohio. June 22, 1864: Rpt. In: *OR*, Ser. I, Vol. 39, pt. II, pp. 137-138. PDF.

7) "Aug. 4th, 1864. Union Generals Squabble Outside of Atlanta." *This Day in History*. History.com. History. 2014. Web. June 24, 2013.

8) Bible, Thomas, Cap. "Military History and Travels of Captain Thomas Bible." Rpt. in *The Blue and Gray: the Federals*. Compiled by Sheila Weems Johnston. Rogersville: Hawkins Co. Genealogical and Historical Society. 1995. p.166-167. Print.

9) Bible in Johnston. 168.

10) "8th Tennessee Volunteer Infantry Regiment." *Tennesseans in the Civil War: Federal Infantry Units.* Tngenweb.org. Rpt from *Tennesseans in the Civil War Vol. I.* 1964 TNGenweb Project. July 14, 2004. Web. 1 June, 2013.

11) "8th Tennessee Volunteer Infantry Regiment." *Tennesseans in the Civil War: Federal Infantry Units.*

12) "8th Tennessee Volunteer Infantry Regiment-USA." *The Blue and Gray: the Federals.* Compiled by Sheila Weems Johnston. 3 vols. Rogersville: Hawkins Co. Genealogical and Historical Society. 1995. p. 230.

13) United States. Department of the Interior Bureau of Pensions. *Full Pension File-Civil War.* "Harris, James P." Inv.#1266.352. 29 May. 1901. National Archives and Records Administration. September 1, 2013. Print.

14) "Eighth Regiment. Company I." *Report of the Adjutant General of the State of Tennessee: of the military forces of the state, from 1861 to 1866.* Ancestry.com. Web. Ancestry.com Operations, 2011. January 9, 2013.

15) United States. Department of the Interior Bureau of Pensions. *Full Pension File-Civil War.* "Harris, James P." Inv. #1266.352.

Chapter Seven: Middle Tennessee

1) Bailey, Anne. "Sherman's March to the Sea." New Georgia Encyclopedia. Georgia Humanities Council. georgiaencyclopedia.org. 2009. Web. August 7, 2013.

2) "Ten Facts about the Battle of Franklin." The Civil War Trust. civilwar.org. 2014. Web. July 18, 2014.

3) Bible, Thomas, Cap. "Military History and Travels of Captain Thomas Bible." Rpt. in The Blue and Gray: the Federals. Compiled by Sheila Weems Johnston. Rogersville: Hawkins Co. Genealogical and Historical Society. 1995. p.169. Print.

4) Rubin, Karen. "Battle of Franklin." Examiner.com. examiner.com. 2 Apr. 2011. Web. January 19, 2014.

5) Bible in Johnston. 169.

6) "Battle of Franklin Animated Map." Civil War Trust. civilwar.org. 2014. June 9, 2014.

7) "19th Tennessee Infantry Regiment K Company." Tennesseans in the Civil War: Confederate Infantry Units. Tennesseans in the Civil War Project. tngenweb.org. 2009. Web. June 20, 2014.

8) "8th Tennessee Volunteer Infantry Regiment." Tennesseans in the Civil War: Federal Infantry Units. Tngenweb.org. Rpt from Tennesseans in the Civil War Vol. I. 1964 TNGenweb Project.

7/14/2004. Web. June 1, 2013. The 8th TN Regiment is in the second line of Reilly's Brigade.

9) Bible in Johnston. 169.

10) Bible in Johnston. 169.

11) "8th Tennessee Volunteer Infantry Regiment." *Tennesseans in the Civil War: Federal Infantry Units.* Tngenweb.org. Rpt from *Tennesseans in the Civil War Vol. I.* 1964 TNGenweb Project. July 14, 2004. Web. June 1, 2013. This feat is marked by an historic marker at the corner of Hillsboro Road and Hampton Ave. in Nashville, Tennessee.

12) Bible in Johnston. 170.

13) Bible in Johnston. 171.

14) Bible in Johnston. 172.

15) United States. Department of the Interior Bureau of Pensions. *Full Pension File-Civil War.* "Harris, Thomas L." Testimony of Thomas D. Collette. 22 Apr. 1887. National Archives and Records Administration. September 3, 2014. Print.

16) Bible in Johnston. 170.

Chapter Eight: Andersonville

1) *"The Prison Camp at Andersonville." The Civil War Series. The National Park Service. nps. gov. 1995. Web. June 5, 2013.*

2) "Elmira Prison." *The Civil War Series*. The National Park Service. nps.gov. 1995. Web. June 5, 2013.

3) "The Prison Camp at Andersonville."

4) Rich, Dean. Phone interview. June 30, 2014.

5) United States Army. "8th Reg't Tenn. Infantry Company I Muster roll for William G. Harris." Mar. and Apr. 1864. Provided by: U.S. National Archives and Records. Print. Also Elsie Samsel gives this information on tape and refers to the Bishop house.

6) "8th Tennessee Volunteer Infantry Regiment-USA." *The Blue and Gray: the Federals.* Compiled by Sheila Weems Johnston. 3 vols. Rogersville: Hawkins Co. Genealogical and Historical Society. 1995. p. 232.

7) "8th Tennessee Volunteer Infantry Regiment-USA." In Johnston. 232. Elsie Samsel on tape identifies McAnally as being present.

8) Samsel, Elsie Winkles. Cassette Tape. July 4, 1987.

9) "8th Tennessee Volunteer Infantry Regiment-USA." In Johnston. 230. Multiple family documents and the Johnston compilation of Civil War records identify William G. Harris, 33 years old, as dying in Andersonville Prison. Muster out rolls from the U.S. Army identify the Andersonville casualty as 24 years old, probably because that age corresponds with some of their own records.

10) United States. Census Bureau. *1870 Census, District 9, Grainger County, Tennessee.* "B.Y. Harris." Ancestry.com. Roll: *M593_1530*; Page: *104A*; Image: *212*; Family History Library Film: *553029*. ancestry.com 2009. Web. June 17, 2013.

Chapter Nine: Aftermath

1) *United States. Department of the Interior Bureau of Pensions. Full Pension File-Civil War.* "Harris, James P." *Inv.#1266.352. 29 May. 1901. National Archives and Records Administration. September 1, 2013. Print.*

2) McGinnis, Robert A. *In Sweet Remembrance: the Cemeteries of Grainger County, Tennessee Vol. III.* 2008. p.143. Print. Richard Bishop fought for the Union in the 4th Tennessee Infantry.

3) *Grainger County, Tennessee and Its People.* Waynesville, NC: Walsworth Pub. 1998. 71. Print.

4) Fisher, Noel. *War at Every Door: Partisan Politics & Guerrilla Violence in East Tennessee, 1860-1869.* Chapel Hill: The University of North Carolina Press. 1997, 157. Print.

5) Fisher. 154.

6) McKenzie, Robert Tracey. "Oh, Ours Is a Deplorable Condition." *The Civil War in*

Appalachia: Collected Essays. Eds. Kenneth W. Noe and Shannon H. Wilson. Knoxville: University of Tennessee Press. 1997. 207. Print.

7) Grainger Co. Book of Deeds for 1865. 15. p. 787.7. Microfilm.

8) Hawkins County, Tennessee, County Court. "Administers Bond and Letter to Bartlet Y. Harris." September 1866. JPG file.

9) United States. Census Bureau. *1870 Census, District 12, Hawkins County, Tennessee*. "James Harris." Ancestry.com. Roll: *M593_1535*; Page: *155B*; Image: *295*; Family History Library ancestry.com 2009. Web. September 7, 2013.

10) McGinnis. 162.

11) Moore, Harry. *A History of the Churches of Grainger County, TN*. Published Grainger Co. Historical Society 1986. 87. Print.

12) *The Bible*. World Publishing: Cleveland. 1981. Print. King James Vers.

13) "Meadow Branch Church of the Brethren, TN." *Brethren Encyclopedia*. The Brethren Encyclopedia, Inc.: Oak Brook, IL. 1983. 805. PDF file.

14) Moore. 85.

15) Moore. 85.

Chapter Ten: Perseverance

1) *McGinnis, Robert A. In Sweet Remembrance: the Cemeteries of Grainger County, Tennessee Vol. III. 2008. 143. Print.*

2) "Inventory and Sale of the Estate of David Harris." 16 April, 1868. Grainger County, Tennessee. Grainger Co. Wills. File # 538. Microfilm.

3) United States. Census Bureau. *1870 Census, District 9, Grainger County, Tennessee.* "B.Y. Harris." Ancestry.com. Roll: *M593_1530*; Page: *104A*; Image: *212*; Family History Library Film: *553029.* ancestry.com 2009. Web. June 17, 2013.

4) *Tennessee State Marriages 1780-2002.* "Bartley G. Harris to Mary C. Harris." Ancestry. com. #918 p.2. Ancestry.com Operations Inc, 2008. Web. 9 Jan. 2013. The exact date is March 28th, 1869.

5) United States. Census Bureau. *1870 Census.* "B.Y. Harris."

6) "Heirs and Wards and Guardianship Settlement Files 1796-1915." *Grainger Co. Probate Court Loose Records.* April 4th, 1870. Microfilm.

7) "Heirs and Wards and Guardianship Settlement Files 1796-1915." *Grainger Co. Probate Court Loose Records.* April 27th -August, 1871. Microfilm.

8) "Heirs and Wards and Guardianship Settlement Files 1796-1915." *Grainger Co. Probate Court Loose Records.* Nov. 27th 1871. Microfilm.

9) *Brownlow's Knoxville Whig.* 8 January 1868. Chronicling America: Historic America Newspapers. Library of Congress. chroniclingamerica.loc.gov. ND. Web. May 21, 2014.

10) McKenzie, Robert Tracey. "Oh, Ours Is a Deplorable Condition." *The Civil War in Appalachia: Collected Essays.* Eds. Kenneth W. Noe and Shannon H. Wilson. Knoxville: University of Tennessee Press. 1997. 210. Print.

11) McKenzie. 210.

12) United States. *Federal Census Non-population Schedule 1850-1880.* "B.Y. Harris 1870 Grainger County." Roll 12, #T1135. 2010. Web. September 21, 2014. Compare to 1860 United States Census "B.Y. Harris."

13) McKenzie. 207.

14) McKenzie. 208.

15) Nelson, Charles. Assistant Director, Tennessee State Library & Archives. Information from *Southern Claims Commission, Disallowed and Bared Claims, 1871-1880.* Email to the author. 7 Dec.2013. The primary document checked on ancestry.com December 9, 2013 was no longer viewable by July 7, 2014.

16) McKenzie. 207.

17) United States. Census Bureau. *1870 Census.* "B.Y. Harris." The blacksmith is B.Y.'s neighbor, who is a renter. Family members recall the red ledger.

18) McGinnis. 162.

19) McGinnis. 162.

Chapter Eleven: Yet Again

1) *United States. Census Bureau. 1850 Census, District 12, Hawkins County, Tennessee. "Peter Barr." Ancestry.com. Ancestry.com 2010. Web. February 3, 2013. Spelled as "Bar" in 1860. Identifying info: Roll: M653_1255; Page: 135; Image: 276; Family History Library Film: 805255.*

2) *Tennessee State Marriages 1780-2002.* "B.G. Harris to Martha L. Barn." Ancestry.com. Ancestry.com Operations Inc, 2008. Web. January 9, 2013.

3) United States. Department of the Interior Bureau of Pensions. *Full Pension File-Civil War.* "Harris, James P." Inv.#1266.352. June 29, 1901. National Archives and Records Administration. September 1, 2013. Print.

4) United States. Department of the Interior Bureau of Pensions. *Full Pension File-Civil War.* "Harris, James P."

5) *Nashville Union and American.* July 29, 1873. Image 3. Chronicling America: Historic

American Newspapers. Library of Congress. chroniclingamerica.loc.gov. ND. Web. May 22, 2014.

6) *Morristown Gazette.* 15 May, 1881. Chronicling America: Historic American Newspapers. Library of Congress. chroniclingamerica.loc.gov. ND. Web. May 22, 2014.

7) Coffee, Ken. "History of Bean Station." *Town of Bean Station.* Town of Bean Station, Tennessee. 2013-14. Web. May 22, 2014.

8) *Moorestown Gazette.* 7 March 1877, image 3 and 16, April, 1879, image 1. Chronicling America: Historic American Newspapers. Library of Congress. chroniclingamerica.loc. gov. ND. Web. May 22, 2014.

9) "Heirs and Wards and Guardianship Settlement Files 1796-1915." *Grainger Co. Probate Court Loose Records.* 1 Apr., 1882. Microfilm. Tutors listed are Lowe in 1871, Hurley in 1872, Garrett in 1874, McCaually in 1875, and Bassell in 1876.

10) United States. Census Bureau. *1900 Census, District 13, Texas County, Missouri.* "William D. Harris." Roll 905 page 11A; Dist. 0139; FHL Microfilm 1240905. Ancestry.com. Ancestry.com 2004. Web. December 20, 2013. The census shows William's daughter born in Tennessee in 1880 and a son born in Missouri in 1883.

11) McKenzie, Robert Tracey. "Oh, Ours Is a Deplorable Condition." *The Civil War in Appalachia: Collected Essays.* Eds. Kenneth W. Noe and Shannon H. Wilson. Knoxville: University of Tennessee Press. 1997. 215. Print.

12) "Productions of Agriculture." p.18. Ancestry. com. *Selected U.S. Federal Census Non-Population Schedules, 1850-1880.* Ancestry. com. Ancestry.com Operations, 2010. Web. December 7, 2013.

13) United States. Census Bureau. *1880 Census, District 2, Grainger County, Tennessee.* "Bartlett Harris." Ancestry.com. Archive Collection Number: *T1135*; Roll: *Roll 23*; ancestry.com 2009. Web. June 17, 2013.

14) Leavitt, Judith Walzer. *Brought to Bed: Childbearing in America, 1750-1950.* Oxford University Press: Oxford. Kindle. 1986.

15) McGinnis, Robert A. *In Sweet Remembrance: the Cemeteries of Grainger County, Tennessee Vol. III.* 2008. 164. Print. Elsie Samsel describes Martha's cause of death on tape.

16) McGinnis, 164. Ap dies July 17,1880, not 1887 as the tombstone transcription says. See also Samsel's MS notes.

17) United States. Department of the Interior Bureau of Pensions. *Full Pension File-Civil War.* "Harris, Thomas L." No. 319125. 5 Sept. 1884.

National Archives and Records Administration. March 10,2014. Print. Date of death March 17, 1881.

18) United States Army. "8th Regiment Tenn. Infantry Company I. Casualty Sheet for Bartley Y. Harris." 28 Nov., 1864. Provided by: U.S. National Archives and Records. Print.

19) McGinnis, 143. Martha dies on November 12th, 1882.

Chapter Twelve: The Trophy Wife

1) *Rich, Dean. Telephone Interview. July 1, 2014. Rich also notes that the house remodel date was ascertained from B.Y.'s home insurance records.*

2) *North Carolina Land Grants in Tennessee, 1778-1791,* comp. by Cartwright & Gardiner. James McCarty land grant. 1788. #2545, 1958. p. 53. Print.

3) "Will McCarty Appointed Captain of Hawkins Co. Militia Nov. 3, 1790." *Territorial Papers of the United States.* Vol. IV. Southwest Territory. Compiled by Clarence Carter. 1936. 437. Print.

4) "Transcription of McCarty Family Bible." *Virginia Genealogist.* Vol. 3 #1. 1959. p. 24. This article contains information missing from the actual Bible housed in the East Tennessee Historical Collection.

5) "Marriage License: Bartley G. Harris and Sarah C. Harris." August 11, 1881. No county. Print. See also *Tennessee State Marriages, 1780-2002,* Hawkins Co. Also, all of B.Y.'s marriages are listed on his Civil War pension material.

6) *Moorestown Gazette.* August 20, 1884. Chronicling America: Historic American Newspapers. Library of Congress. chroniclingamerica.loc.gov. ND. Web. May 22, 2014.

7) *Maryville Times.* 21 November, 1894. Chronicling America: Historic American Newspapers. Library of Congress. chroniclingamerica.loc.gov. ND. Web. May 22, 2014.

8) *Morristown Gazette.* 13 September, 1882, Image 3.

9) United States. Census Bureau. *1900 Census, District 2, Grainger County, Tennessee.* "Barton Harris." Ancestry.com. ancestry.com. 2009. Web. September 2, 2013. All three children's birthdates are clear from this census.

10) McGinnis, Robert A. *In Sweet Remembrance: the Cemeteries of Grainger County, Tennessee Vol. III.* 2008. 164. Print.

11) McGinnis. 166.

12) A History of Tennessee. *The Tennessee Blue Book.* tn.gov. The State of Tennessee. 35. PDF

Chapter Thirteen: The Wheat Thrasher

1) Barnard, Roy Dean. "Winkles" unpublished. Nd. #105.1. Print.

2) United States Army. "Discharge Papers— Brutus S. Winkels." Print.

3) *The Huntsville Daily Times*. 3 June, 1915. p. 7. Chronicling America: Historic American Newspapers. Library of Congress. chroniclingamerica.loc.gov. ND. Web. May 22, 2014.

4) Coffee, Ken. "History of Bean Station." *Town of Bean Station*. Town of Bean Station, Tennessee. 2013-14. Web. May 9, 2013.

5) Currence, Nancy Shaver. Personal Interview. July 22, 2012. Also multiple family sources.

6) *Tennessee State Marriages, 1780-2002*. "Brutus S. Winkels." Ancestry.com. Ancestry. com Operations Inc, 2008. October 30, 1905. Web. July 22, 2014.

7) Samsel, Elsie Winkles. Cassette Tape. July 4, 1987. On the 1900 Census they are in Grainger Co. but by 1910 they are living in Bent, Colorado.

8) United States. Census Bureau. *1910 Census, Bent, Colorado*. "William D. Harris." Ancestry. com. Roll: *T624-112* Page: *13B*; Enumeration District: *0004*. FHL microfilm:1374125 ancestry.com 2009. Web. July 22, 2014.

Chapter Fourteen: Last of the Embers

1) Moore, Harry. *A History of the Churches of Grainger County, TN*. Published Grainger Co. Historical Society 1986. 85. Print.

2) Receipt from Isaac Morris. October 12, 1901. MS.

3) Murray. J.B. Letter to B.Y. Harris. October 30, 1915. MS.

4) United States. Census Bureau. *1930 Census, District 2, Grainger County, Tennessee*. "Brutus Winkels." Ancestry.com. Roll: *2247*; Page: *11A*; Image: *326.0*; FHL microfilm: *2341981*. District 2 2002 Web. July 22, 2014.

5) "Settlement of the Estate of B.Y. Harris." By B.S. Winkles. Grainger County, Tennessee Court. March 27, 1920. TS.

6) Measuring Worth Calculator for 2012. measuring worth.com. Web. May 7, 2014. The amount given is in 2012 U.S. dollars.

7) Deed. B.Y. Harris to Brutus Winkels. *Grainger County, Tennessee Book of Deeds Vol. 44*. p. 559. June 1916. PDF.

8) Samsel, Elsie Winkles. Cassette Tape. July 4, 1987. While several family members referenced this letter, a copy of it does not survive.

9) McGinnis, Robert A. *In Sweet Remembrance: the Cemeteries of Grainger County, Tennessee Vol. III*. 2008. 164. Print. B.Y. makes the

comment about the corpse in a letter to Sam, Will, and their families.

10) United States. Department of the Interior Bureau of Pensions. *Full Pension File-Civil War.* "Harris, James P." "Declaration for Widow's Pension." Inv.#1266.352. 29 June, 1901. National Archives and Records Administration. September 1, 2013. Print. James dies two years later in Missouri. Booker died in 1908, also in Missouri.

11) McGinnis. 164.

The David and Polly Harris Family

David T. Harris and Mary (Polly) Lansford married Dec. 21st 1816 in Pittsylvania Co. VA. His parents are Thomas and Rebecca Harris; hers are Isham and Mollie Lansford.

Their Children:

---Elizabeth b. Oct. 26, 1817, VA. Marries William A. Long 1861. Dies July 25, 1888. Bur. Long Cemetery, Grainger County, Tennessee.

---Rebecca b. 1820, Pittsylvania Co., VA. Marries Peter G. Meek Feb. 8, 1848. Dies Grainger County. Bur. Meadow Branch Cemetery, Grainger County, Tennessee.

---Thomas L. b. 1822. Marries Susie Tinker. Dies Mar. 16, 1881. Bur. Long Cemetery, Grainger County, Tennessee.

---Mary Lansford b. Aug. 27, 1824 in VA. Marries Almarine M. Wynkel (Winkel) Feb. 1, 1844. Dies 1882, buried in Grainger Co. Almarine Wynkel was born Oct. 1818, Green Co. TN. Dies Hancock Co. TN in 1893.

---Bartlet Yancy (also called Bart and B.Y.). b. Nov. 25, 1826, Pittsylvania Co., VA. Dies Oct. 15, 1919. Bur. Meadow Branch Cemetery, Grainger Co., Tennessee (See Appendix #2 for information on his wives.)

---William G. b. 1829, North Carolina. Marries Mary Gray ca. 1856. Dies Jan. 1864, Georgia.

---Booker M. b. 1832, North Carolina. Marr. Eliza T. Lansford and later "Mary." Dies in Newton Co., Missouri in 1908.

---Susan W. b. 1834, Virginia. Marries James B. Harris. Nov. 29, 1855, Grainger Co., Tennessee. Dies Grainger County, Tennessee.

---James Parmenas (Jim) b. Mar. 17, 1836, TN. Marr. Margaret E. Gray prob. Hawkins Co., TN. Nov. 4 1858. Dies Bates County, Missouri, February 28, 1922.

---Richard B. b. 1840 Grainger Co., Tennessee. Dies 6 Aug. 1864, Atlanta, Georgia.

B.Y.'s Wives and Children

(Unless otherwise noted, all events take place in Grainger County, Tennessee. Much of this information is taken from Samsel's notes.)

Lucretia A. Gray:
b. Mar. 1827 prob. Hawkins Co.; Marr. Sept. 23, 1852 in Hawkins Co.; dies Nov. 15, 1866.

---William David, b. Nov. 30, 1853 in Grainger or possibly Hawkins County, Tennessee; Marr. Maggie Brooks (Matilda); dies 1941 in McClave, Colorado.

---James Thomas, b. Aug. 26, 1857; Marries twice. Dies June 28, 1928.

---(Mary) Louisa, b. July 29, 1860. Marr. John W. Gammon. Dies July 17, 1897.

Mary Gray Harris:

b. Mar. 1827 prob. in Hawkins Co.; Marr. Mar. 28, 1869 prob. in Hawkins Co.; dies Sept. 20, 1871.

---Jacob B., b. June 10, 1871; dies Dec. 22, 1871.

Her children with William G. Harris were probably all born in Hawkins County, Tennessee: Sarah Harris, b. 1858, Catherine Harris, b.1859, Rebecca Harris, b.1862 (or Dec. 1861).

Martha L. Barr:

b. Oct. 11, 1850 prob. in Hawkins Co.; Marr. Jan. 28, 1872.; dies July 10, 1880.

---John Fredrick, b. Mar. 21, 1873; dies Nov. 14, 1894.

---Porter Simeon, b. July 28, 1875; Marr. Ida Bell Isenberg Dec. 25, 1904; dies Dec. 15, 1947.

---Cora E., b. Jan. 13, 1878; Marr. Robert F. Winkel Aug. 1891; dies Mar. 26, 1955 in Fruita, Colorado.

---Ap Malsbee, b. May 13, 1880; dies July 17, 1880.

Sarah (Sallie) Catherine Webb:

b. Dec. 12, 1852 in Hawkins Co.; Marr. Aug. 11, 1881 in Hawkins Co. Dies Feb. 22, 1919.

---Samual E., b. Oct. 30, 1882. Marr. Elsie Ure 1907 in Colorado. Dies May 2, 1944 in Emmett, Idaho.

--- Grace Quinter, b. May 14, 1885. Marr. Bruce Seabern Winkels Nov. 1905. Dies Jan. 15, 1963.

---Yancy Bartlet, b. June 9, 1888. Marr. Sept 1911 Dixie Wright. Dies Jan. 19, 1919.

Harris and Bean Station/ Mooresburg Men in Company I of the 8th Tennessee Volunteer Infantry Regiment

Thomas L. Harris, age 43, B.Y.'s older brother, enlists July of 1863.

Bartlet (B.Y.), age 36, enlists on March first of 1863. Wife's name: Lucretia Gray.

William G. Harris, 33 and B.Y.'s next youngest brother, joins on January 13, 1863. He is married to Mary Gray, Lucretia's sister. A company roll has him mustering in on June 30th and transferring to Company I August 1st.

James P. Harris (Jim), age 28 and B.Y.'s younger brother, also signs up on March 1st, 1863. He is married to Margaret Gray, Lucretia's youngest sister.

Richard B. Harris, age 23, joins January of 1863. B.Y.'s youngest brother, he is referenced in Joseph Bare's letter home.

Relatives in the 8th Tennessee:

Almarine M. Wynkle (Al), age 44, joins January of '63. He is a husband to B.Y.'s sister Mary.

David T. Harris, age 32, joins in early July. He is a cousin.

Peter Meeks is referenced in Bare's letter home. He is husband to B.Y.'s sister Rebecca.

CPSIA information can be obtained
at www.ICGtesting.com
Printed in the USA
BVOW09s1048291017
498948BV00019B/308/P